HOW TO
BECOME A

CONTESTANT:
An Insider's Guide

HOW TO

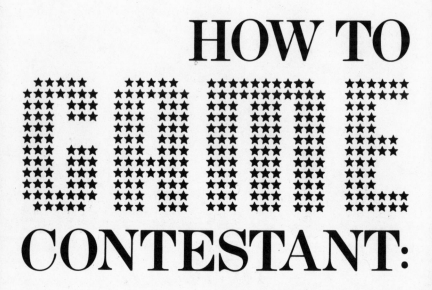

CONTESTANT:

GREG MUNTEAN AND

FAWCETT COLUMBINE

BECOME A SHOW

An Insider's Guide

GREGG SILVERMAN

• NEW YORK

This book is dedicated to

A.A.C.
ALL ASPIRING CONTESTANTS

Where trying's a necessity
and winning's an attitude

A Fawcett Columbine Book
Published by Ballantine Books
Copyright © 1987 by Greg Muntean
and Gregg P. Silverman
Foreword Copyright © 1987
by Alex Trebek

All rights reserved under International
and Pan-American Copyright Conventions.
Published in the United States by
Ballantine Books, a division of Random
House, Inc., New York, and simultaneously
in Canada by Random House of
Canada Limited, Toronto.

Library of Congress Catalog Card Number:
86-92117

ISBN: 0-449-90268-4

Cover design by James R. Harris
Book design by Alex Jay/Studio J

Manufactured in the United States of America
First Edition: August 1987
10 9 8 7 6 5 4 3 2 1

CONTENTS

Foreword by Alex Trebek   ix

Introduction   xi

1. "For $50,000 and the Car..."
   The Contestants' Perspective   2

2. "For $50,000 and the Car..."
   The Insiders' Perspective   20

3. Romantic Winners
   For Love and Money   42

4. Know Your Game   54

5. The Audition   88

6. "On the Set of..."
   Hollywood Game Show   98

7. Know Your Talent   116

8. Myth...Understood   158

9. Address for Success   168
   Game Shows   177
   Talent Shows   202

ACKNOWLEDGMENTS

From Greg Muntean

Mom (Sally Muntean), I love you for your constant love and support during the creation of this book and throughout my life.

Dad (Ted Muntean), your living being was with me during the preparation of this book and I know your spiritual love and support are giving me the strength to succeed.

Uncle Charlie and Aunt Katie (the Chetons), thank you for loving me as one of your own.

Debra (my best friend Debra Fisher), thank you for seeing me through the harder times.

Mary and Mrs. Morar (Mary Henderson and her mother, Anna Morar), thanks for insisting that I apply for employment at Merv Griffin Enterprises.

To all my friends at "Wheel of Fortune," You're Beeeaaauutiiifulll!

Gregg (my coauthor), thanks for your days, nights, middle of the nights, sitting at the computer and watching the printer spit out page after page after page ... while I was contestant-searching cross country. And thanks for your creative juices ... I wouldn't have been able to do it without you.

From Gregg P. Silverman

Tony Frascone, Kessa, Minkie, Nina, and Moscow: Thanks for your love, purrs and undaunted attention.

Mom (Maggie/Marian Silverman), thanks for your strength to persevere—your listening ears. I hope this book is an inspiration to your own creative fantasies.

Dad (Sidney Silverman), thanks for backing me through thick and thin ... And for being there to praise me each time I made it.

Marsi and Eric, Scott and Michelle, Stacy and Jon (my siblings and siblings-in-law), all my successes I share with you and your children.

Uncle Allen (Allen Magdovitz), thanks for seeing me through my rough and "Smooth Moves."

Evelia and Omar, te quiero mucho.

Greg (my coauthor), thanks for adding a new dimension to my life ... with your sense of wit, your thinking style, your personality and your friendship. Thanks for tolerating my off-the-wall brainstorming in the most inappropriate places and at the most unimaginable times.

From Greg and Gregg

Merv Griffin Enterprises, thank you for serving as our mentor.

Alex Trebek and the staff of "Jeopardy!", thanks for your continued support.

To the game show industry and its talented people, thanks to all of you—without you this book wouldn't be possible.

The accounting firm of Ernst & Whinney, thank you for your invaluable research; your expertise made the "Myth ... Understood."

Tanya Maxwelle, thank you for the crisis intervention.

Laurie Golden (Jacob's Well, Public Relations), thank you for your idea for the format of the book ... and your other creative ideas, as well.

Foreword by Alex Trebek

At the end of every "Jeopardy!" program the comment I most often hear from the contestants is one of relief. "I'm glad I didn't make a fool of myself." In an age of proliferating VCRs, people want to record their special moments and they certainly don't want to appear foolish. They want everyone to see them at their best in the right setting.

If there is one thing that the last couple of years have demonstrated, it is that television game and quiz shows, led by the phenomenal success of "Wheel of Fortune" and "Jeopardy!," are enjoying a resurgence. I don't think it is an accident that these two shows have become the most popular programs ever in first run syndication. What they excel at is involving the viewers. They virtually compel you to play along and match your skills against the contestants in the safe, no-risk environment of your home.

For some people, they also provide the added thrill of competing for cash and prizes before an excited live audience and with the knowledge that millions more are watching all over the country. What a marvelous high for those of you who love to compete and show off. But there is a catch.

Game shows are very much like the Great American Dream. If you have the right combination of desire, skill, luck, and opportunity, you too can be rich and famous. However, without them your chances of being a winner on television or in life are slim indeed.

What this book will do is provide you with enough information about the various game shows so that you will be able to assess accurately your own level of desire to compete.

Since skill is acquired, the book will instruct you in ways to practice and polish your techniques for competition. Some elements of luck are beyond your control, but there are ways to get the most out of the situation by realizing your full potential and making your own luck. Opportunity is one of those nebulous elements that seems to present itself most often to those who are in the know and prepared. Even if you never try out for a game show, with this book you'll acquire an insight that should add greatly to your understanding and enjoyment of these programs.

For those of you who make it past the testing and appear on television, you should remember that you are there to have fun. Understand also that everyone associated with the show wants you to succeed and win big. The show thrives on winners, so enjoy the moment and keep it in its proper perspective. You are not there to change the world political or economic situation. You are there to fulfill Andy Warhol's prediction. You will be a star.

INTRODUCTION

Setting: The New Hollywood Library
GREGG SILVERMAN: "Excuse me, are you using this periodical index?"

PROFESSIONAL–LOOKING MAN IN A SUIT: "No . . . go ahead, I just found the statistics I needed for the chapter I'm on."

GREGG S.: "Chapter for what? I hope you don't mind, but I was glancing at your notes and noticed some of the terminology. I'm curious. What are you working on?"

MAN IN SUIT: "I'm a corporate lawyer writing a book on the problem of achieving self-actualization in the difficult eighties."

GREGG S.: "That's great! I'm coauthoring a book on a similar topic . . . how to get on a game show."

MAN IN SUIT: "What? You've got to be kidding."

GREG MUNTEAN (*Yelling across the library*): "GREEEGGG! I FOUND THE FIFTH SOURCE WE NEEDED TO BACK UP THE STATISTIC THAT ONE HUNDRED MILLION TV VIEWERS WATCH GAME SHOWS WEEKLY."

GREGG S.: (*Yelling back across the library*) "THAT'S GREAT!" (*turning to man in suit*) "Now we've got the final statistics we need for our introduction."

MAN IN SUIT: "One hundred million people watch game shows weekly?"

GREG M. (*approaching*): "I've been reading statistics in every major periodical for the past year, but I had to validate the number for myself ... between the ten million would-be contestants for the total game show industry and the 75,000 I've interviewed during my career it's mind-boggling. Maybe I'm just too close to it."

GREGG S.: "That's why I'm your objective outsider. (*Turning to the man in the suit*) This is my coauthor, Greg Muntean, the contestant coordinator for 'Jeopardy!' and before that, 'Wheel of Fortune.' Greg, he's a corporate lawyer writing a book on self-actualization in the difficult eighties."

GREG M.: "With these statistics, getting on a game show should make an easy first at the top of your self-actualization list."

MAN IN SUIT: "I just could never fathom why anyone would risk making a fool out of himself on television."

LIBRARIAN: "Greg and Gregg, I found another resource for you... does that mean that you'll get me on 'Jeopardy!'?

GREG M. (*Turning to man in suit*): "Fools? These people are stars of the most widely viewed shows in the history of television. And what they can earn for their brief stint of stardom ranges from consolation prizes that would save anyone a bundle at the grocery store to more than $1,000,000."

GREGG S.: "And one of the most emotional memories of their lifetime. As an author writing a book on a heavy psychological topic, I assume you're aware of one our era's most-quoted social commentators, Andy Warhol, who said, 'The day will come when everyone will be famous for fifteen minutes.'"

GREG M.: "Here's some key information from our book (*Reading from clipboard of notes*): More than one hundred million TV viewers watch game shows weekly. There are more than 650,000 contestant auditionees a year. The competition is stiff; therefore, your preparation process has to be thorough—you must become a master of your game and personality.

"There's a big difference between winning big at home during bites of your sandwich and trips to the kitchen, and competing against fifty other would-bes in a high-pressure audition situation. And then—playing your game off a huge fluorescent playing board on an actual set in front of five cameras, a studio audience and blinding lights, while being taped for viewing by more than fifty million, including everyone you know and love."

MAN IN SUIT: "How does your book help people to become contestants?"

GREG M.: "Our book is a comprehensive guide to becoming a contestant on your targeted game or talent show. We break down the contestant process and offer you a systematic and enjoyable approach to becoming a contestant. Contestant coordinators' number one frustration is the lack of qualified contestants. We are constantly amazed at how many of these intelligent would-be contestants lose out because they are unprepared—they don't know their game and don't display their best personality. Due to the increasing numbers of auditioning contestants, preparedness is not a luxury, it is a necessity. 'I

INTRODUCTION

didn't know what they expected of me,' is the typical comment of the long-faced rejected would-be contestant. There is no longer room for this excuse. You now have the insider's perspective on what is expected of the potential contestant."

MAN IN SUIT: "I never really looked at becoming a contestant from those angles. I knew the game show industry was big business, but I didn't understand the numbers. After listening to the two of you and reading these notes I'm tempted to put becoming a contestant at the top of my actualization list. I might even interview you for my book. I could probably better address the issue if I knew what it was like to be a contestant. I know, why don't you get me on 'Jeopardy!'?"

GREG M.: "Why don't you read our book?"

HOW TO
BECOME A

CONTESTANT:
An Insider's Guide

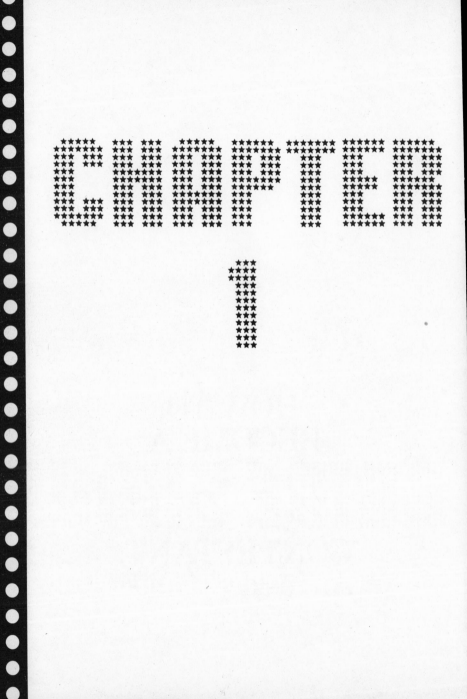

CHAPTER

1

"FOR $50,000 AND THE CAR..."

The Contestants' Perspective

"My best friend dared me! My friend, Andrea, said, 'Why don't you go on a game show?' I laughed it off. She persisted, called and made the appointment at the 'Super Password' office. I watched the show every day. I went through the initial interview, was asked back for a second meeting, and then was asked to report to the next taping session two weeks later. It was a difficult two weeks. At times I felt confident. Those feelings lasted only two seconds. Then insecurity surfaced. I thought, 'I'll freeze up...I'll act stupid ...I'll look stupid...I am stupid.' To make a long story short, I won $53,600 on 'Super Password' and it was wonderful to play with Betty White. It was unbelievable when I won. The whole experience was unforgettable. It was scary but I'm proud that I did it."

—Leslie Gershman

Would you do it? Would you subject yourself to:
- ...fifteen minutes of stardom?
- ...national television debut in front of millions of people?
- ...being seen by friends and relatives all over the world who haven't been in touch for years who suddenly call to say, "I couldn't believe it was you on TV!"?

- ...financial security for years?
- ...a brand, spanking new car WITH NO PAYMENTS?
- ...a video cassette that you'll cherish for the rest of your life?

You might be thinking "television's television, we all know it's staged. People like me really don't win big."

"If I can get picked anyone can get picked. As I sat watching myself on television, my three-year-old daughter was just shocked. She kept saying, 'Mommie, Mommie, why are you on TV and sitting here watching TV with me?' I think one of the reasons they picked me was because I said I was a housewife...besides being bubbly. I couldn't stand still. This is what happened! My two girlfriends and I got tickets to 'The Price Is Right' that day and went to the studio. They told us that just because we had tickets didn't mean we would even get in to be part of the audience. Only about 300 out of about 450 got in. First they gave everyone a number, then they had us stand in another line, and then they interviewed five people at a time and asked me only about two questions. 'What do you do for a living?' I told them I was a housewife in San Diego. And they asked me, 'Where is San Diego?' I said it was south by Tijuana. That was it. Next thing I knew I was sitting with the rest of the audience when they said, 'Kym Joseph, come on down!' I went flying out of my chair as if someone stuck me with a pin. I was jumping around at the podium—I couldn't stand still. It took me five chances to finally get up on stage...can you believe, it was by $1.00. I won the first round and a dinette set on stage. I was talking with Bob Barker...kissed him...and told Bob that my daughter and I watch the show every day. I went back to my seat...And then I couldn't believe I was called back for the big spin. When they said, 'Kym, you're the winner,' I was in shock. I couldn't believe I won. I couldn't believe I went all the way up to win $15,000 more in prizes including a cruise to Alaska. It happened so fast. To this day, I never once thought about being on television."

—Kym Joseph

"Outside in line I didn't have any expectations. I didn't feel any different than I always felt. I felt if anyone would get picked it would be my wife. She's more outgoing than I am, a bubbly kind of person. But I felt if anyone could answer the questions it would be me. I watch 'The Price Is Right' quite often—three or four times a week for the last nine years.

★ 7 ★

Lawrence Adams in a winning
moment on "The Price Is Right."

"In line, I was paying attention to what the producer was asking. He asked me what my name was and what kind of work I do. I said I'm retired. He asked me what I was retired from? I said, work. He said what kind of work? I said all kinds. I knew what he was getting at—it was a nice conversation between the two of us. There were a lot of people out there and he had to select only a few.

"I won the first round. I won a sailboat. Then for the grand prize I guessed the cost of a camera ...I have a number of cameras. I knew pretty well what the price range was and I got to try to unlock a safe to get the car. I was shocked—I felt good—but I was shocked. It tests you...you have to pay attention to what's being said by Bob Barker and whoever else is saying it. And if you get all flustered and lost in the process...you're gonna lose it. They don't have time to cover you and baby you. You only have a few minutes up there and you have to make those few minutes count. The one thing I learned as an army officer is sometimes you have to do it quickly.

"It made a believer out of me. I was one of those people who didn't believe these things were real. But it's for real."

—Lawrence Adams

How did Leslie do it? What did Kym and Lawrence do and say right? "If I can get picked, anyone can get picked!" Sounds great, but why do the Leslies get selected out of thousands of others going through the very same interviewing process? And why do the Kyms and Lawrences get picked out of an anonymous lineup of hundreds of people? Is it their career? Their brain? Their hair color? Their outfit? The acting lessons? Who they know? Or could it be *what* they know?

"My first game show attempt was 'The Match Game' in 1978 and I was rejected. I remember perfectly. I tried to be as sophisticated as can be. Like a model on TV I was very polite and played the game. They never called me.

"For 'Card Sharks,' I had watched and played the game at home. The interview was in the same place as 'The Match Game.' At first, I got nervous because it brought up the old experience. But once inside, I was positive and confident from watching the show for five months solid—and I had planned to be myself. I knew I was going to have fun, there was an energy in the room. I made it feel as if I walked into a room of my best friends."

—Susie Guidi

"I tried out eight times for different shows and didn't make it. I went to the interview for "Sale of the Century" and there were over 120 people there. I watched the show daily. I taped it or had someone tape it if I couldn't watch it.

"I heard people at the interview asking each other how this game is played. I heard people say that they couldn't make it to the second interview. I heard people saying, 'What did they say?' You have to pay attention. I listened to everything that was told to me. I did not chitchat. I listened to the contestant coordinator. I listened to the producer. I listened to the prize lady."

—John Gose

$80,000, four trips including one month to South America, a new car, and more than $8,900 in jewelry later, John had listened well. The prize lady should be flattered.

Susie in her new Cadillac and John in his new 300 Turbo ZX are both still riding high on their winnings...big winnings.

Besides the spanking new cars, what else do Susie and John have in common? Winners of big money...yes!!! Winners of stardom...yes!!! Winners!!! But they didn't end up as winners— they started out as winners. They came to the game show experience with the WINNING ATTITUDE.

John Gose, second from right, celebrating his earnings on the "Sale of the Century."

JOHN: "They gave me the opportunity to do my second interview in the afternoon after my first interview. I went and had my one suit dry-cleaned and changed into it for the interview. One of the show's people asked me, 'Didn't you have something else on earlier?' For the chance of my lifetime, I was going to give them my best."

SUSIE: "At the second interview, inside I felt as if I was in Las Vegas when you pull the handle and you're waiting for the last number to click. I was excited. I could feel it and I knew they could feel it. Everyone was cheering on the others ... everyone was extremely real."

HOW'S YOUR WINNING ATTITUDE?

You've watched your favorite game show for years, for so long that cobwebs materialize on the couch during *your half hour*. With little or no jealousy (a little bit is good for the competitive edge), you've cheered on thousands of contestants while they jump around on stage winning thousands of dollars, new cars, trips to the Caribbean. You get nine out of ten answers correct. You know the contestant address flashing on the screen by heart.

Cheryl Reinwand, after winning big on the "$100,000 Pyramid."

"I had been thinking about it for a year. I had watched "$100,000 Pyramid" so long—off and on for fifteen years—I figured I could do it. The first try–out they said I wasn't good enough, to go practice and come back in three months. I waited six months. In fact, during those six months, I watched every day. I would write a list of words that they used. Then, later in the evening, my husband and I would practice the words. I played much better at the next interview. I could tell that they noticed me."

—Cheryl Reinwand

Cheryl Reinwand won $150,800 and a trip to the Fiji Islands on the "$100,000 PYRAMID."

"I used to watch the show when I was a kid, age five or six. I remember it from then. Then, when "Jeopardy!" came back on I started to watch it again. At school, we would sit around at dinner and watch the show. The show was doing a contestant search in Detroit and they announced it on Michigan TV. I tried for two hours on the telephone. It was busy the whole time, but I finally got through.

"I have a broad background in a lot of subjects and did college bowls in college. During the in-

Chuck Forrest buzzing in
on "Jeopardy!"

terview, I was fast on the buzzer. It helped a lot in terms of speed. In fact, I got an electronic buzzer system from the college bowl people and hooked it up for practice. I bought the home version of the game. I continued to play with friends. You must think like the writers. I watched for hints in questions, beat out the others on the buzzer and broke their concentration."

—Chuck Forrest

Chuck Forrest won $172,800 in cash on "JEOPARDY!"

Are you ready to buzz in?
. . . to take a risk; possibly the most memorable risk of your life?
. . . to experience the unbelievable excitement and thrill of being on national television?
. . . to practice for the most pleasurable money you'll ever make?
. . . to bare yourself for a toaster?

Host Alex Trebek
congratulating Chuck.

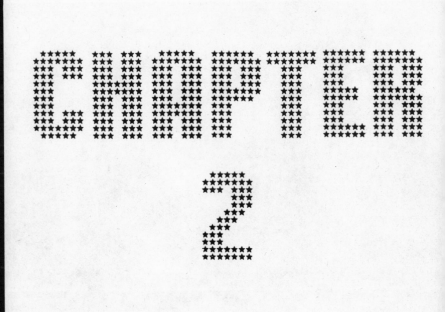

"FOR $50,000 AND THE CAR..."

The Insiders' Perspective

Bob Eubanks, host of "The New Newlywed Game."

"Everyone is on your side. Share your natural humor and your natural emotions. The worst thing you can ever do is not be yourself. The moment you start acting and not being your soul is the moment everyone starts turning off to you. That's what makes the show look phony. That's why we don't use actors. The show only works if it's pure. *You must truly like to bare yourself for a toaster!* Contestants that give us phoniness put us in jeopardy."

    —Bob Eubanks, Host of "The New
    Newlywed Game" and "Card Sharks"

"We're looking for natural contestants, natural character, including sweet people. Phony contestants stand out. We're not looking for faking or phoniness. Be yourself."

    —Roger Dobkowitz, Producer, fifteen years
    "The Price is Right"

"Just be yourself. If you act as a game show contestant 'should' act, it's not realistic. Have energy that's real, not false! I look for people who can play the game, not plastic beautiful people who will look great on TV."

    —Fred Westbrook, Contestant
    Coordinator, three years
    Industry credits: "The New Battlestars,"
"Your Number's Up," "Crosswits"

"The more honest and direct you display your own personality, the better you will be as a contestant. Be yourself!"
—Bob Stewart, Executive Producer,
"$25,000 Pyramid," "$100,000 Pyramid"
"Chain Reaction," and "Jackpot"
Industry credits: Creator of the "Pyramid"
shows, the original "Price is Right,"
the original "To Tell the Truth,"
the original "Password," "Jackpot,"
and "Chain Reaction"

"Emphasize your strong points! Be positive in your attitude! Remember that this is probably the only time in your life that you will be on national television in front of thirty million people. The best advice I could give contestants would be the line from a popular television commercial for the Armed Forces—'Be all that you can be!' "
—Alex Trebek, Host of "Jeopardy!" and
"Classic Concentration"

"Know your game. Ninety-nine percent of what we look for is game-playing skills in terms of fast players; players that know the rules. You don't

"Jeopardy!" host/producer Alex Trebek

have to be a cheerleader. Be the best game player that you can be!"

—Lisa Furuboten, Contestant
Coordinator, two years, "$25,000
Pyramid" and "$100,000 Pyramid"
Industry credits: former contestant on
"$25,000 Pyramid," winner of
cash and a trip to Tahiti

" . . . a crackerjack game player with energy, enthusiasm, loud clear voice. KNOW THE GAME! Never try out for a game show you haven't practiced or ever seen. BE YOUR BEST. Dress as though you were going to a job interview—clean, neat, not too casual. Present yourself with confidence and good humor; have the ability to give good, supportive, positive reinforcement to your fellow players."

—Tony Pandalfo, Contestant Coordinator,
more than ten years
Industry Credits: Contestant Coordinator
for "Celebrity Talk," "Chain Reaction,"
"Jackpot," "Wheel of Fortune,"
"All Star Blitz," "$10,000 Pyramid";
former contestant on "$10,000 Pyramid"
—winner of cash

"For your best personality, think of flirting with someone. *Flirting brings out the best in everyone.* It's the best key to unlocking the personality of someone. Not just flirting, it's the idea of flirting to capture someone's eye, to capture someone's attention. Your true identity shows, the real person in you."

—Elaine Joyce, Host,
"The All New Dating Game"

Chuck Barris Productions

Elaine Joyce, on the set of "The All New Dating Game," demonstrating how "flirting brings out the best in everyone."

"Don't sit quietly! If you don't like to see yourself boring like boring contestants on TV, don't be boring. How do you imagine yourself on television? Project that in your interview. Be uninhibited, quick-witted, express yourself, show yourself, give energy and enthusiasm. This is your one shot."

—Walt Case, producer, "The All New Dating Game" and "The New Newlywed Game"
Industry credits: Producer of "You Bet Your Life," "The Toni Tennille Show," "All Star Secrets," "Guinness Game," "Stumpers," "Rhyme and Reason," "Treasure Hunt," original "Dating Game," original "Newlywed Game"

"Make the experience fun! While you're at it don't dwell on the money and prizes you might win. You don't need that added pressure. Play the game for the audience, the producers, the contestant coordinators in exactly the same manner you played it while watching at home and saying to yourself, 'I can do that!' Well do that! Be yourself, live it up, and enjoy your chance to shine!"

—Wink Martindale, Host, "High Rollers" Producer, "Bumper Stumpers"

Wink Martindale,
host of "High
Rollers"

"The camera has an absolute way of disclosing the real person. Show your winning personality. Be outgoing, vivacious, positive! Talk positive! Be yourself by treating the person you're talking to—the host or the other contestants—as a friend. Don't mumble, have a gripping handshake, don't use monosyllabic words or slang. The person auditioning you wants you to qualify; the more people he or she finds the better. He or she wants you to win."

—Dan Enright, Executive Producer,
Barry & Enright Productions
Industry credits: Forty years Creator or
co-creator of "Tic Tac Dough," "Twenty-
One," "The Hollywood Connection,"
"Concentration," "People in Conflict,"
"Crossfire," "Winky, Dink and You"
and many more; Executive Producer of
"Joker's Wild," "Joker, Joker, Joker,"
and many more

"Everyone watching thinks that they should be in your shoes; they want to think that you're having a great time. If you emanate sincerity and warmth it will give you the winning edge. Act like it's your own living room. That's not to say, don't be excited. You should show your enthusiasm and warmth. *Smile with a Capital 'S.'* NO ONE WANTS TO WATCH A BORE."

—Ben Vereen, Host, "You Write the Songs"

"You Write the Songs" host
Ben Vereen with contestant.

Ken Sax

"Be anticipatory—as if you're about to be a part of a terrific adventure. If the couples enjoy each other's company and appreciate each other's qualities and you reveal this attitude during the audition, I can feel it...and I'm quite likely to want to see you again! We're looking for support and warmth between couples.—Couples that can relate to each other as loving people. If couples criticize each other, they will not be on the show."

> —Jerry Modine, Contestant Coordinator, two years, "$1,000,000 Chance of a Lifetime"
> *Industry credits:* Contestant Coordinator, eight and a half years "Family Feud"

"We're all here to make some money for you, but you're to have a good time while we're doing it. Relax! I know it's difficult with all the people running around, the cameras, the lights, people telling you what to do, remembering all the rules. It's not easy. I tell the contestants on my show, "Hollywood Squares," to take a deep breath, sit back and relax! *Don't forget—you're there to have fun!!!*"

> —John Davidson, Host, "Hollywood Squares"

"Hollywood Squares" host John Davidson.

Helping a contestant "have a good time."

"Smile a lot…have a great attitude. We're looking for spunk. Be friendly to other contestants. We like seeing everybody supporting each other and having a fun time on the show. But also look like you're having fun! A lot of people say they're having fun, but don't show it on camera."

—Beth Fiance, Contestant Coordinator, two-and-a-half years, "Scrabble"
Industry credits: former cash-winning contestant on "Scrabble." She was UCLA's representative during College Week.

"Hang loose, have fun and show it! You must have vitality. But don't overthink. You're there to have fun."

—Edythe Chan, Contestant Coordinator, "Jackpot" and "Chain Reaction".
Industry Credits: Contestant Coordinator with Bob Stewart Productions, twenty-five years. "Chain Reaction," "Jackpot," original "$10,000 Pyramid" and more: Producer, three years, of "Eye Guess"; Associate Producer, eight years, original "Price is Right"

"Go with the flow of it all. Show the true sense of fun. You're not competing with the other contestants. Express yourself, be real, be honest, but don't try to compete. Don't be boring. Have fun!"

> —Jeffrey B. Scharping, Contestant Supervisor, two years, "The All New Dating Game" and "The New Newlywed Game"
> *Industry credits:* Page for NBC; production assistant at Disney Channel

"The contestants that do the best are the ones who want something different in their lives. Yes, they want money and prizes, but they're the ones who go in for the real fun experience. They're happy when they win, they're happy when someone else wins. They have 'real' fun."

> —Andrea Carroll, Contestant Coordinator, five years, "Sale of the Century"
> *Industry credits:* Talent Agent, four years; assistant to casting director—specialty Commercial Casting, three years

"Being a game show contestant is a thrilling lifetime experience. *Whether you win big or win a ceramic dog, every contestant's a winner...*

Contestants showing the "true sense of fun" on

"The New Newlywed Game."

"Wheel of Fortune" host
Pat Sajak and Vanna White.

winner of lifelong memories. In fact, the video cassette recording of your game show experience will be played at your every birthday party for the rest of your life!"

—Pat Sajak, Host, "Wheel of Fortune"

"People have been finding long-lost relatives and friends through watching the show (Jackpot)."

—Doug Gahm, Producer, "Jackpot" and "Bumper Stumpers."
Industry Credits: Producer at Global Television, five years, "That's Life," "Pizzazz," and more

"Being a contestant is a fantasy fulfillment. It's an everlasting memory. You'll tell your kids. You are the stars of the shows. Think of what you like about contestants and do it. It's a once-in-a-lifetime experience. How do you want to be remembered?"

—Michael Hill, Producer, more than twenty years
Industry credits: currently producing the number one game show in Germany; Producer of "All Star Secrets," "Guinness Game," "You Bet Your Life," the original "Dating Game," and the original "Newlywed Game"

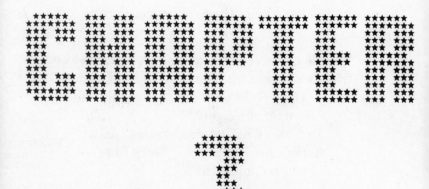

CHAPTER 3

ROMANTIC WINNERS

For Love and Money

If you had your choice of prizes between a lifetime mate or a microwave oven, which would you choose?

Eleven years ago Cheryl and Bill Gilmore made their love selection with a wedding and the beginning of a love partnership that would lead them to becoming a $1,000,000 couple—$40,000 a year until the year 2011. In February of 1986, Bill and Cheryl used their strong relationship to become millionaires on the "$1,000,000 Chance of a Lifetime":

CHERYL AND BILL: "Our relationship was cemented before we went on the show. A peace fell over us a year before the show. We truly believe that this show was the reward of our great relationship. With all the problems that we did have, we finally found peace. We did that ourselves and somebody was rewarding us for getting this far."

CHERYL: "But getting to the taping itself was a feat."

BILL: "Let me tell you what happened. I didn't find out about the interview until a week before. Cheryl had made the appointment, but had kept it a secret. Well, on the day of the audition I forgot all about it. I walked into our trailer at 3:10.

Cheryl called the show and got the time extended. To make a long story short, with grease covering my body from work, I had to change my clothes on the freeway on the way from Bakersfield to Hollywood. We walked in, shook hands (grease and all), and the person in charge announced that she wanted everyone 'bright and bubbly.' I said to Cheryl, 'Let's get the hell out of here.' She begged me to stay."

CHERYL: "I told him, 'Bill, all you have to do is press the buzzer.' Seven days later, they called us back for a second interview, and again I told Bill that all he had to do was press the buzzer. This time he pressed, and it didn't work. Bill was embarrassed, the producer said it was OK and it was uphill from there."

BILL: "I knew in my heart that I was not going to be able to answer anything. At the taping, Cheryl was a cat on a hot tin roof. She couldn't stand still. For weeks she felt pressured to win!"

CHERYL: "At one point before the taping, Bill grabbed me and said, 'We're here to have a good time. We've had a free meal, met a lot of nice people. It doesn't matter [if we don't win]. It worked. The first two games it was me against the board. I could feel Bill behind me giving me *energy sup-*

$1,000,000 Chance of a
Lifetime, XPTLA Company,
Photo by Michael Leshnov

New millionaires Cheryl and
Bill Gilmore with "$1,000,000
Chance of a Lifetime" host
Jim Lange.

port through me to the board. By the third game I was competing against a smart couple. By the time I got to the $1,000,000 bonus round, I wound down. Bill was holding me up. I was almost burnt out by this point. In the booth we both answered the final answer together with one second left on the clock. I went numb.

BILL: "Jim Lange said, 'You did it!' I heard the other contestants in the back going wild. All of a sudden, Cheryl was going down. Her knees gave out, she almost fainted. Nothing in the world mattered. I reached out for her and we staggered out of the booth."

CHERYL: "I don't remember what happened. Bill was expressing all the emotions I wanted to express. He was guiding me through the crowd. He was my leaning post for a couple of days."

CHERYL AND BILL: "Never in our lives had we been the center of attention. We had had a small wedding with a preacher and six friends. It was the first time we had a mass celebration."

Bill and Cheryl's eleven-year strong love selection grew into a bond strong enough to use their love and mutual support to win $1,000,000.

The new Mr. and Mrs. Mansour (Kerri and Michel) had just acquired each other as lifetime mates and they decided to test their new partnership on "The New Newlywed Game":

KERRI AND MICHEL: "We fought all the way back home after we lost. We had lost everything, all the questions. But we did make everybody laugh. They told us to say anything we wanted, so we were spontaneous, we elaborated...so we lost."

KERRI: "I think they called us back for the alumni of losers because we made everybody laugh. Me with my high voice—like Cyndi Lauper, and Michel with his Arabic accent. This time we studied the questions they might ask."

MICHEL: "This time we picked a great vacation as a prize preference, a strategy we both agreed on. When we won, Kerri jumped on me. We almost fell backward. I felt much closer to Kerri because we did something great together and won together!!!"

KERRI AND MICHEL: "It was a fifty-fifty project. Other people put us on a pedestal. In Jamaica, six different couples from all over the states

knew us from "the Newlywed Game." They
would say, 'Aren't you the ones from "The Newlywed Game?" We thought you were great on TV.'
It made us feel like celebrities."

Richard and Lee Ann Kelley started off their relationship being celebrated. In fact, they were a
match made on TV in a soap-opera-like situation
that can only happen on a game show. The winning ingredients:
- the right game show...
- the right two people...
- the right setting...
- add more than a pinch of fate...
and you have "The Love Connection!"
    Richard and Lee Ann Kelley announced their
engagement on the air—on "The Love Connection" show—only three weeks after Richard, the
selector, made his initial telephone connection
with his choice of a date, Lee Ann, from the three
selectees.

LEE ANN: "It seemed like ages when the show finally called to update their file on me: 'Was I still
available, etc. etc. etc.' (After watching the show
every night for years, what did he think my answer would be?) Yes! Yes! Yes! I knew something
was up. A few days later the show's matchmaker,

Richard and Lee Ann Kelley's "Love Connection" wedding.

Brad, called me to say that someone would be calling me for a date. He had picked me. I pumped Brad for info, including how big of a nerd is he—no luck with answers—but begged him with the major question, 'Is He Taller Than Me?' (I'm 5' 11") and Brad said yes. I breathed a little easier."

RICHARD: "Can I talk now? The four telephone conversations before our actual date—five hours of date planning and getting comfortable over the phone—helped, but like no other date I can remember, when the night arrived, everything got screwed up... and that doesn't happen to me. I accidentally washed my wool tie (it shrunk). I got tied up in traffic, searched for a pay phone off the freeway to announce I was going to be late, and if that wasn't enough, I got offered a paper bag at my first meeting (she was polite enough to cut holes out for my nose and eyes). Can you believe, the first thing she hands me when I walk in is a paper bag? She tells me I look like her ex-husband. And says you don't look thirty-four, you look forty-four. I knew, I really did, that our sparring was fun and good (those five hours on the phone helped), but I was still insecure."

LEE ANN: "I was done up—a 4:30 hair appointment and I never do that for anyone. A new dress, new shoes, and I had requested a coat-and-tie guy. Richard fit the bill. Just one puzzlement; all night Richard had not made a move. Through slow dancing, romantic dinner, etc. At my house, on my couch, towards the end of the evening I made the first kiss."

RICHARD: "Other than sharing the two kinds of soup we ordered at dinner and her first advance on the couch, she had not given me any indication that she was into the date. When I finally kissed her goodnight I said, 'We're going out again. Don't worry about it, we're going out again.'"

LEE ANN: "And I said, 'Yeah, but I won't accept!'"

Lee Ann called the next day to ask Richard out!

Richard and Lee Ann broke all the rules of "Love Connection" by going out every night before their reappearance on the show three weeks after the first date...when they announced their engagement on the air.

KNOW
YOUR
GAME

(riiiinnnnnggg)

"Betty, I just saw a Cheryl Reinwand win $100,000 on the 'Pyramid.'"

"Cora, what's a Cheryl Reinwand?"

"She's a rich woman...I should be so rich. I played just as well at home as she just did. What was her secret...She had to have a secret."

When we asked Cheryl Reinwand the same question, what her winning secret was, she quickly answered, "It's no secret. I worked hard for it. I watched the show every day and wrote down the list of words they used, including backup clues. Later in the evening, my husband and I would practice, going over the game every evening. There's no way anyone can say I didn't earn that money. It was hard work."

Winning is a strategy. It's not a fluke that these big winners win or got on game shows in the first place. These people charted their game plan for the game show of their choice—no "eenie meenie minie moe pick a channel and that's the show" for them.

STEP I:
TARGETING YOUR GAME SHOW

Winning contestants preplan the game show of their choice. Each game show falls into a specific category requiring certain game-playing skills. First, you must study the categories. Winning

Stars of the trivia/quiz
show "Hollywood Squares."

contestants then select the right category geared towards their game-playing abilities. The final step: selecting the specific game show that they play the best, have the most potential to win, and enjoy the most. It should be a labor of fun.

A. THE GAME SHOW CATEGORIES

There are four categories which cover all game shows of the past, present, and future:

1) Trivia/Quiz
2) Word/Puzzle
3) Personality
4) Kids/Teens

Category 1: Trivia/Quiz

Trivia/Quiz game shows test your general knowledge of, but are not limited to: people; current events; history; politics; sports; business; entertainment; geography; religion; and products, as well as your ability to recall this knowledge in a designated time frame format.

Trivia/Quiz Game Shows	Contestant Status
"Card Sharks"	individual contestants
"High Rollers"	individual contestants

Contestants demonstrating the winning spirit

on trivia/quiz show "Jackpot."

Trivia/Quiz Game Shows	Contestant Status
"Hollywood Squares"	individual contestants
"Jackpot"	individual contestants
"Jeopardy"	individual contestants
"The Price is Right"	individual contestants
"Sale of the Century"	individual contestants
"Split Second"	individual contestants

Category 2: Word/Puzzle

Word/Puzzle game shows test your knowledge of vocabulary, language, puns, homonyms, antonyms, grammar, sentence structure, phrases, famous quotations, and plays on the alphabet. The different game shows in this category use one or more of the above word and/or puzzle themes in their own specific playing formats.

KNOW YOUR GAME

Word/Puzzle Game Shows	Contestant Status
"Bumper Stumpers"	two individuals team
"Chain Reaction"	individual contestants
"The $1,000,000 Chance of a Lifetime"	married couples
"Classic Concentration"	individual contestants
"The $25,000 Pyramid"	individual contestants
"The $100,000 Pyramid"	individual contestants
"Scrabble"	individual contestants
"Super Password"	individual contestants
"Wheel of Fortune"	individual contestants
"Wordplay"	individual contestants

"College Week" on the word/puzzle game show

"Wheel of Fortune."

Category 3: Personality
Personality game shows test your spontaneous responses—including your unedited display of emotions—to your own personal experiences and real-life situations.

Personality Game Shows	Contestant Status
"The All New Dating Game"	single individuals
"Love Connection"	single individuals
"Love Me, Love Me Not"	single individuals
"The New Newlywed Game"	newly married couples (two years or less)
"Truth or Consequences"	individual contestants
"Win, Lose or Draw"	individual contestants

Face to face for the first time on the personality
show "The All New Dating Game."

Category 4: Kids/Teens
Kids/Teens game shows are specialized shows and game show industry events catering to individual contestants under eighteen years of age. These shows cross over each and every game show category depending on the shows currently on the air and the special game show events celebrating kids/teens.

Kids/Teens Game Shows	Contestant Status
"Double Dare"	two individuals/team
"Puttin' on the Hits"	solo or group
"Puttin' on the Kids"	one or more individuals/ solo or group
"Star Search"	one or more individuals/ solo or group

Juniors and Teens Divisions Special Events	Contestant Status
"All New Dating Game"	single individuals

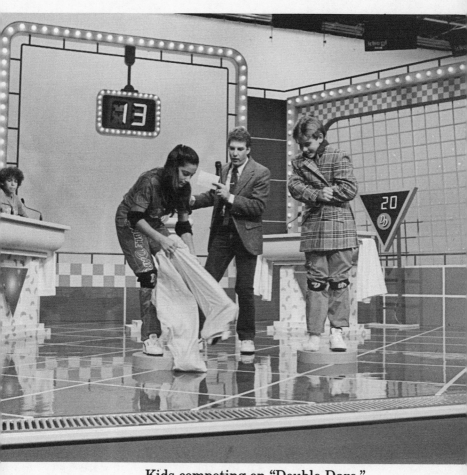

Kids competing on "Double Dare."

Juniors and Teens Divisions Special Events	Contestant Status
"Card Sharks"	individual contestants
"Jeopardy"	individual contestants
"Sale of the Century"	individual contestants
"Scrabble"	individual contestants
"Truth or Consequences"	individual contestants
"Wheel of Fortune"	individual contestants

B. SELECTING YOUR CATEGORY

What are your best game-playing skills? Where are your strengths? It's easy to determine if you've been playing trivia games since you were knee-high—you'd go for the Trivia/Quiz category. If you tackle the Sunday *Times* crossword puzzle every week with a vengeance, you'd gravitate toward the Word/Puzzle category. Do you thrive on attention and are you constantly "on" with others? If "show biz" is in your blood, you'd satisfy your urge with the Personality category.

There are games you can play at home to help you determine and hone your own particular skills. Choose from this chart to help you along.

TRIVIA/QUIZ

Board Games:
Trivial Pursuit
Jeopardy
Sale of the Century
Quizzard
Alumni Fun
Any miscellaneous trivia/knowledge games

Traditional games:
twenty questions

Books:
Super Trivia Encyclopedia
Games: The Book of Sense and Nonsense
books on general trivia
books on riddles
books on quotations

Periodicals:
One major newspaper daily to keep abreast of
current events (i.e., *The New York Times*,

Washington Post, Los Angeles Times, USA Today, Chicago Tribune)
Newsweek, Time, People, U.S. News & World Report

Video/computer/arcade games:
"Rapid Fire Memory Challenge Game" (Video)
"Flash Match" (Video)
"Eye Witness Newsreel Challenge" (Video)
"Official TV Game Show Program—Jeopardy!" (Computer) Software for Apple II and Commodore
"Sports Trivia" (Computer) software for Commodore 64 and 128
"Entertainment Trivia" (Computer) software for Commodore 64 and 128
"Master Trivia" (Computer) software for Commodore 64 and 128
Any trivia/quiz games (Arcade)

WORD/PUZZLE

Board games:
Wheel of Fortune
Scrabble—traditional
Scrabble—game show version
The $1,000,000 Chance of a Lifetime
Upwords
Boggle
Any miscellaneous word board games

Traditional games:
hangman
ghost

Books:
Games: Book of Crossword Puzzles
Games: Book of Games
Games: The Book of Sense & Nonsense
The New York Times Crossword Puzzle Book
The Scrabble Puzzle Book
The Dell Crossword Dictionary
The Word Game Winning Dictionary
Word Power Made Easy
books on homonyms
books on puns
books on antonyms
books on crossword puzzles
major unabridged dictionary
major thesaurus

Periodicals:
Your local newspaper's crossword puzzles and
        word games
major newspaper's crossword puzzles and
        word games
TV Guide weekly crossword puzzle

Video/computer/arcade:
video—any word/puzzle games
computer—any word/puzzle games
arcade—any word/puzzle games

PERSONALITY

Board games:
The All New Newlywed Game
The New Dating Game
any games involving spontaneous verbal
    communication

Traditional games:
charades

Books:
books on public speaking
books on extemporaneous speaking
books on improvisational acting
books on acting in front of the camera

Video:
Rich Little's Charade Game
Honeymooner's Game

KIDS/TEENS

Kids and teens will use the same tools for preparing for a game show as the three other categories. Because the kids/teens category is more limited in its selection of shows, it's best to choose your game show first, then find out what category it belongs in. Use the chart to prepare for the game show of your choice.

To gain the full benefit of your Game Show Preparation Chart for the particular tools you require, consult toy stores, libraries, book stores, magazine/newsstands, video stores, computer accessory stores (software).

After studying your game show preparation chart, do you know which category is right for you? If you're still not sure, take a piece of paper and place these three categorical headings at the top.

Trivia/Quiz　　　Word/Puzzle　　　Personality

Answer each of the questions below in as much detail as you can and put your answers underneath the category they belong. When you're done, add up the number of answers under each category. The category with the most answers will be your winning category.

- What type of games: do I play best? am I quickest at? do I enjoy the most? do I feel most comfortable playing? have I been playing the longest? do I win most at? do I feel most competitive about? do I play most regularly?
- When I play games, am I more interested in the mental skills of playing the game or the social/conversational aspect of playing with others? under intense pressure?

C. SELECTING YOUR GAME SHOW

You have rated your game-playing interests and skills and game-winning track record. Once you feel confident with your game show category, IT'S TIME TO TARGET YOUR GAME SHOW.

Begin by watching all of the game shows in your selected category. You will first notice that each game show has a unique format, different personality energy levels and a variety of winnings. Now that you have assessed what you are going to bring to the game show you ultimately choose, it's time to ask yourself: What is it I want from my game show?

- What do I want to win? prizes, money, a date?
- Do I want to play individually or with as-

signed teammates (other contestants or celebrities)?

- How far do I have to go for the audition? Does the show conduct contestant searches near my hometown? (See the Address For Success chapter for complete details).
- How fast-paced is the show's format?
- What time is the game show on television in order to accommodate my own schedule and my soon-to-be-adopted game-show-watching practice sessions?

STEP II:
BECOMING AN EXPERT
AT YOUR GAME SHOW

By getting to this point in the book, you have made the commitment to work towards what may be the most profitable few days in your entire life. Becoming an expert at your game show and winning is hard work, but perhaps the most pleasurable work you'll ever get to do. As Cheryl, the "$100,000 Pyramid" winner, emphasized, "There's no way anyone can say I didn't earn that money...it was hard work." But what she went on to say was, "I enjoyed every minute of it. I wouldn't trade a second of it."

A. WATCH YOUR GAME

Watching and familiarizing yourself with your targeted game show is the key ingredient to becoming a contestant. You MUST watch your game on a regular basis, preferably daily. Plan to be at the television as your game show begins, with few or no distractions. If you are unable to watch it at its regularly scheduled times, use a video cassette recorder to tape your show. What to watch closely for:

The basic playing format of the game. The format is how you, as a contestant, play the game. For example, on "Wheel of Fortune," you spin a wheel and call a consonant. Your goal: complete a word/puzzle. On "Jeopardy!" the question/answer format of a trivia/quiz show is reversed and the host delivers an answer on a subject. Your goal: provide the correct question to the answer. On "The All New Dating Game," the contestant selector asks one of the three contestant selectees a hypothetical question. Your goal: a creative spontaneous response capturing the attention of the selector.

The rules of the game. The rules are the proper procedural components governing the format of the game. They dictate the way you, as a contestant, MUST play the game. For example, on

★ 78 ★

"Wheel of Fortune," once you spin the wheel, you MUST give a consonant to help you complete the word/puzzle. Another rule: you MUST have $250 in your "bank" in order to buy a vowel. On "Jeopardy!" you MUST deliver your answer in the form of a question. Another rule: you MUST wait until the answer is read by the host before you buzz in or you could be locked out of that "answer/question." On "The All New Dating Game," the selectees MUST remain behind the partition, out of view from the selector. Another rule: the selector MUST have prepared his or her questions so that they are brief and to the point.

The language. The language of the game consists of the actual words and expressions—the lingo—used by the game show as part of the playing format of the game. You are encouraged to use your particular game show's lingo or your chances of becoming a contestant are slim to none. You MUST play in the spirit of the game. For example, on "Wheel of Fortune" you'll hear contestants enthusing, "Come on $5,000" while the wheel is in motion. And when they're ready to take a stab at the answer, they make their request by saying, "I'd like to solve the puzzle."

B. PRACTICE THE GAME
John Gose, the $160,000 "Sale of the Century"

winner, Susie Guidi, the $33,000 "Card Sharks" winner, and Chuck Forest, the $175,000 "Jeopardy!" winner all became experts because they studied and understood the format and rules of their games. They spoke the language of their games fluently; it became second nature to them. They played as experts before they played for winnings.

Three Key Ways to Practice and Prepare for Your Game

1. Play along with the game regularly while watching the game:

   a) Cover up revealed answers on the screen (use masking tape, turn your chair around), *ensure* that you cannot see the answer and that the answer is not audible prior to your own answering along.

   b) Always write your answers down—have a pen/pencil and paper with you at every viewing session. Each day, add up your correct answers to monitor your progress.

   c) Practice the language and expressions of the game—the specific words, the volume and emotional expressions.

2. Create a mock version of your game:

   a) Using your furniture, create a functional game-playing situation similar to the show itself. You might even want to simulate on-the-set conditions by playing the game with bright lights and slightly distracting background noise (such as a radio news broadcast) to strengthen your concentration.

b) Use your family members, roommates or friends to play the game with you. Choose people whose game playing skills exceed yours. When you play against someone who is better than you, you work harder.

c) Develop your own trivia quizzes, puzzle tests, and hypothetical questions using your show's current games as guidelines.

3. Use the tools from your preparation chart:

a) If games similar to your game show are available, play them on a regular basis—be it the actual board game of your show, another board game similar to your show, a video game, an arcade game, or a game printed in a periodical. Try different mediums, switching from one to another.

b) Use the other tools—specialized books, periodicals, and informational vehicles—to develop a variety of skills needed for your game.

STEP III.
DEVELOPING YOUR TELEVISION
GAME SHOW PERSONALITY

Imagine you audition hundreds of people every day for a starring role in "your" game show: What kind of contestants would you look for? Contestants who attract attention, contestants who shine, contestants who will keep the viewer from changing the channel, contestants who express real emotions...real people.

YOUR PRESENT STRONG PERSONALITY AND APPEARANCE TRAITS
Where would you stand in your own audition... what would you notice about yourself? Circle the personality and appearance traits that best describe you.

PERSONALITY	APPEARANCE
outgoing	contemporary hairstyle
shy	wear heavy makeup
easygoing	wear no makeup
nervous	wear light makeup
mellow	sharp dresser

PERSONALITY	APPEARANCE
friendly	half smile
reserved	full smile
verbal	gleaming eyes
quiet	defined figure
use eye contact	erect posture
amusing	unique facial
serious	expressions
conversationalist	clear complexion
assertive	
optimistic	
sensitive	
apologetic	
unique laugh	
noticeable hand gestures	

● WHAT FIVE PERSONALITY AND AP-
PEARANCE TRAITS THAT YOU CIR-
CLED ABOVE HELPED YOU TO GET
YOUR LAST JOB?

- WHAT FIVE PERSONALITY AND AP-
PEARANCE TRAITS THAT YOU CIR-
CLED ABOVE HELPED YOU GET YOUR
LAST DATE?

- WHAT FIVE PERSONALITY AND AP-
PEARANCE TRAITS THAT YOU CIR-
CLED ABOVE ARE YOU ALWAYS
COMPLIMENTED ON BY FRIENDS AND
STRANGERS?

MY POSITIVE PERSONALITY TRAITS	MY POSITIVE APPEARANCE TRAITS
1) _____	1) _____
2) _____	2) _____
3) _____	3) _____
4) _____	4) _____
5) _____	5) _____

You can capitalize on your five strongest personality and appearance traits when you audition.
In addition to your own unique strengths, you'll
need the following:

a) A good speaking voice. Enunciate your words and speak up in a loud, clear voice.
b) Be articulate. Express your thoughts in complete sentences using words familiar to your vocabulary.
c) Eye contact. When communicating with someone or when someone is communicating with you, use your eyes to indicate your sincerity in what you are saying and interest in what other parties are saying.
d) Express enthusiasm. Be interested in the activities. Be interesting—share yourself in a positive, fun manner. And *smile*.

COMBINING YOUR PERSONALITY AND APPEARANCE TRAITS WITH YOUR GAME-PLAYING PRACTICE

"I was excited. I didn't really have to act. When I play a game, I want to win. But I did make an extra effort when I was at the interview. I sat up straight in my chair. I would lean forward in the chair at the right moments, expressing real enthusiasm. I wasn't giggly, but I felt the giggly had a better chance than the quiet. I would lean forward when I spoke, open my eyes wide. I made eye contact with the interviewers. I projected. I spoke loud enough—not yelling—I wanted the person across the room to hear me as if we were standing next to each other. I knew I wasn't going to get picked for my looks. I was going to have to overcompensate for my looks. And I also knew my game, which was my strongest overcompensation. I watched the "Wheel" for six months. I played intensely. You just can't talk to me while I'm watching the game. I played it out loud and I informally instituted a mock game when friends came over. They had to join in, otherwise commercial time was the only time they got my attention.

Mona Najimy won $29,000 worth of prizes on the "Wheel of Fortune."

Play it with personality!
● Play along with the game with the energy and enthusiasm auditionees would need to get picked. Watch the winning contestants in action. If your game calls for applause, applaud with real emotion and excitement. If your game calls for cheering for other contestants combine the language with facial expressions and hand gestures. If your game calls for standing on your head, stand on your head.
● Create a mock interview for your audition—it's your turn to tell your mock game players your life story. Prepare a brief autobiography unique to your personality, interests, rare ex-

periences, distinct accomplishments, and special career involvements. Stand up, speak clearly, articulate, let your personality shine, emphasize eye contact, and express real enthusiasm. Smile when you feel a smile. Believe and feel what you are saying about yourself. How do you want millions of viewers to remember you?

KNOW YOUR GAME
Practice Chart

a) X - I watched the show!
b) X - I drilled myself on my game playing skills!
c) X - I set up a mock version of the game!
d) X - I practiced the language of the game!
e) X - I rehearsed my personality skills!

	S	M	T	W	TH	F	S
week 1							
week 2							
week 3							
week 4							
week 5							
week 6							

CHAPTER
5

THE
AUDITION

SALLY'S AUDITION DAY

The alarm went off promptly at 7:30 A.M. and an immediate excitement rushed through me as I suddenly realized what today was—my audition for "The Win of Your Life" at 10:30 A.M. I turned on the coffee maker, headed for the closet to choose between the two outfits I'd debated over for days. Will it be the new dress I bought that seemed perfect for the audition or the blue outfit that I'm always complimented on? Maybe I should wear my hair differently, and dress up my makeup so I look more dramatic, more movie-starrish.

Wait a minute, I know my game. I've practiced for months. I know my personality strengths and have worked on them. I know what works best for me. I know what feels most comfortable. I love my blue dress, I like the way I do my makeup, and the way I do my hair. Why change everything now when I need to be the best and most confident "me" I have to be?

I finally find a parking space, look at my watch. It's 10:15. Great. At least I don't have to jog the two blocks to the place. But my pace is swift, because I'm excited—nervous—but excited. My head spinning with thoughts of what it's going to be like. Before I walk into the building, I get rid of the gum. I check in with a secretary who thumbs through pages of names. I sigh with relief when she finds mine. I fly down the hall towards the audition room, bursting with energy.

I feel my face drop when I enter the room filled with more than fifty other would-be contestants ...people who must all be wearing their new outfits, new dos, and vying to be a star. Well, Sally, you're not a star, but you are an expert at your game and you know your best personality... shine!

I take a seat and fill out the application and personality profile form. I had done a mental run-through on the way to the audition. I knew what I wanted to write. I was the most honest and sincere "me."

As I finish writing about the funniest thing that ever happened to me, someone passes me another form. I turn it over and panic—a page full of puzzles. I feel the same sense of dread as when I took my driver's license test, that algebra test in eleventh grade, those pop quizzes in history. O.K. Sally, don't panic! I take a deep breath. I close my eyes and make a mental picture of watching my game show. I remember how well I did on yesterday's puzzle, open my eyes, look at the puzzles with a new surge of confidence and think to myself that these are just like the puzzles I've been solving for months.

THE AUDITION

"Good morning everybody, my name is Ted, and I am the contestant coordinator for 'The Win of Your Life.' How do you think you did on your puzzle test?"

Well, does he want an answer or not? Obviously not, because he immediately starts reciting a list of names.

"Scott Marsina*...congratulations, we'd like you to stay for the second interview, Stacy Jonerica* please join Scott, Michelle Jessian* we're pleased to have you stay..."

Where's my name...WHERE'S MY NAME...This isn't fair! I know I did well. Or maybe I didn't...well I thought I did...

"Sally Cheton*...Sally Cheton, are you still with us?"

I can feel myself snap out of my temporary overdramatic daydream. And now my name is being repeated. I smile one of my brightest and say thank you as Ted puts his clipboard down and bids his cordial farewells to the others. I promise myself that I will be all ears until I bid my last farewells.

"Welcome to the second audition. As you can see you are part of a select few. Are you all ready to play the game?"

---

*Not their real names.

He motions for us all to applaud in unison with his bright smile plastered on his face as his eyes sweep through the group. He starts looking my way (eye contact, Sally, confidence). His eyes hit mine and I make sure my eyes show my real excitement and the real "me."

Ted calls up groups of people to play the game. I am getting nervous. I am in the next group. O.K. Sally, don't panic! I take a deep breath, close my eyes and picture myself in my living room playing at my own mock game...my mind flashes on the format, rules, and language...they come to mind as if they were second nature.

"Sally Cheton."

This time my name is only called once. My mind is flooded with thoughts. O.K. Sally, this is what you've practiced months for. I stand up and feel everybody's eyes on me. I walk to the front of the room.

"We're looking for your game-playing skills, your energy, and enthusiasm. It's not whether you win or lose, we're looking for good players with personalities that you would like to see on television. Relax! Now, let's play 'The Win of Your Life.' "

O.K., I know the format, language, and the rules. I'm going to pretend that these people are in my living room playing my mock game with me.

"Sally Cheton, stand up and tell us a little something about yourself!"

Wait a minute, I thought I was done. O.K Sally, don't panic, I've been practicing my interesting stories, I know what I said at my last job interview. I know what body language I use that grabs people's attention. I take a deep breath, and I speak from my heart.

I sit down and anxiously await the results. As a surge of optimism sweeps through me, I think that print dress won't gather mothballs in the closet after all. I can wear it to the taping.

"Thank you for coming. You all played great! If you don't hear from us within the next three weeks, keep practicing and come back in six months. We'll be happy to see you then."

O.K. Sally. Three weeks dedicated to phone-sitting won't be all that bad. Even six months isn't that long!

"To answer your question, sir, no one leaves the audition knowing if they are going to be on the show, even though you passed the test, you played the game, and you had a personality interview with us. We see hundreds of people each week, we

can't possibly use everyone. But thank you for auditioning for 'The Win of Your Life.' "

Two weeks later.
(riiiiiinnnnnng!)
"Hello, Sally Cheton... this is Ted from 'The Win of Your Life'... Good news!"

THE WIN OF YOUR LIFE
SAMPLE CONTESTANT APPLICATION

NAME _____ SS# _____

ADDRESS _____

CITY _____ STATE ___ ZIP _____

HM/PHONE (_____) _____ WK/PHONE _____

VISITING? WHERE STAYING _____

TEMP/PHONE _____ HOW LONG _____

OCCUPATION _____ EMPLOYER _____

AGE _____ MARRIED _____ #OF/CHILD/GRAND _____

BIRTHPLACE _____ HOMETOWN _____

EDUCATION _____ SCHOOL(S) _____

HOBBIES/INTERESTS _____

FUNNIEST MOMENTS _____

SPECIAL ACHIEVEMENTS/INVOLVEMENTS _____

MEMBER OF ENTERTAINER UNIONS? _____

ANY AFFILIATION WITH OUR NETWORK _____

IF SO, LIST NAME/RELATION _____

LIST ALL GAME SHOWS ON WHICH YOU HAVE APPEARED:

DATE _____ SHOW _____

DATE _____ SHOW _____

DATE _____ SHOW _____

AVAILABILITY _____

I CERTIFY THAT TO THE BEST OF MY KNOWLEDGE, THE
ABOVE INFORMATION IS TRUE AND CORRECT.

DATE _____ LEGAL SIGNATURE _____

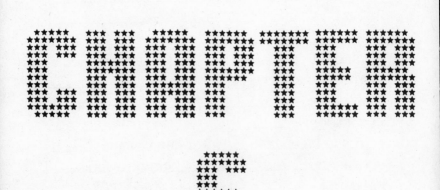

CHAPTER

6

"ON THE SET OF..."

Hollywood Game Show

SALLY: "I can't believe it! You're kidding. You mean I'm coming to Hollywood to be a contestant on 'The Win of Your Life'?"

TED: "That's right, Sally! You're one of the chosen, kid. Grab a pencil and some paper and I'll give you all the details. We want you for February 24th and 25th; plan to be there for both those dates because we tape five shows a day. The reason we need you for both taping days is that the selection of contestants for each particular taping is done just prior to each show. Therefore you could be slated for the first show on the first day of taping or the tenth show on the second day of taping. We're calling you a month in advance so you can make all necessary travel arrangements. We recommend The Stars Inn which gives discounts to our contestants. O.K. Sally:

- Your arrival time: Arrive at the studio gate at 12:00 noon and check in with the guard. He'll have your name and he'll direct you to the contestant lineup where one of my staff will greet you.

- What to wear: Wear your first taping outfit to the studio and bring four changes of clothing in case you're a five-day champ. Do not wear or bring any solid black, solid white, or small stripes as they irritate the cameras. We tell our male contestants that our show prefers ties and sport jackets, and for our female contestants we suggest that you wear dresses or skirts.

- Your guests: We have reserved five tickets for any of your relatives or friends you would like to have in the audience. Please tell them to go to the studio's east gate at 2:00 P.M. where they will check in with one of the studio's pages.

"Sally, please call us the day you arrive in Hollywood. Next time I see you, you'll be in front of five cameras and a studio audience playing 'The Win of Your Life.'"

SALLY: "Ted, I can't wait. Thanks for choosing me. You'll be proud of me. Just wait and see, I'm going to practice night and day for the next month."

February 24th, 12:00 Noon

I rushed up to the studio guard gate with my garment bag filled to the brim with my four outfits. There were already seventeen other contestants lined up outside the gates with their cleaners' plastic bags and other clothing paraphernalia in their arms. I was wearing my good luck print dress for my first taping. Every outfit I brought had something familiar about it and gave me the confidence that had gotten me this far. I'm not typically superstitious, but I go with what works for me.

I felt the energy, the excitement shared by these special people—soon-to-be contestants. As Andy Warhol would note, our fifteen minutes of stardom was soon to be granted.

12:30

An attractive woman from inside the gates approached the group and introduced herself as Dina, one of the assistant contestant coordinators. And the group immediately bombarded her with questions. She laughed almost haughtily, welcomed everyone to Hollywood and the studio, and motioned for the guard to let everyone through. We played follow-the-insider through the maze of a Hollywood studio lot. I was in awe of the whole setting. I had goosebumps.

12:45. The briefing.

The room was bubbling with energy!

TED: "Good morning everybody and welcome to Hollywood and 'The Win of Your Life.'"

ALL OF THE CONTESTANTS IN UNISON: "Hi, Ted!"

TED: "I know you have many questions, all of which will be answered during this briefing session. First I want to congratulate all of you on being selected as contestants and tell you, on behalf of 'The Win of Your Life,' we're proud to have you as the stars of our show."

I felt a mixture of excitement, nervousness, anticipation, and stimulation. The room was filled with an aura of phenomenal energy. There was something magical going on in the green room— Lights, Camera, Action. Stardom, short-lived as it may be, would soon be ours.

Ted's briefing was definitely detailed. I had no idea the legal ramifications of being a game show contestant. Who would think?

- *Security* coverage from the moment you leave this room to the moment you leave the studio. Generally, move as a group; unless for any reason one must make an emergency telephone call or absolutely have to use the bathroom. Do not talk to other people in the studio, not even in casual conversations. Stick to your group. Only talk to the group, other key people from 'The Win of Your Life,' and the TV network people (i.e., security). If you have any problems, ask for assistance.

- *No guarantees* that everyone will appear on the show even though all have arrived at the studio assuming they will be on the show. The game show has the legal right to refuse appearance. There are several reasons for this harsh reality:

1) Game shows always bring in more people than they need in case someone gets sick or someone doesn't show up. Most likely, extra people will be carried over to the next taping or a future taping. In some cases, extra contestants are considered standbys for these special situations.

2) During the rehearsal, the contestant coordinators are still watching for energy and game-playing ability. If for any reason they feel that one will not function well on the air, they may refuse your appearance. It is *not* a contestant's right to be on a game show; it is a privilege.

3) If it becomes known that you are acquainted with someone at the studio, even under innocent circumstances, you could be cut from the show. Example: An old school chum of yours works a camera in the studio, which could constitute a conflict of security rules and you would be disqualified.

4) Security is broken by leaving the group, talking to others, or disruptive conduct. While at the studio, you are under tight security similar to jury duty; don't share the game show "case" with anyone. Broken security means the party's over.

TED: "You will receive a more comprehensive briefing on the set from our TV network security people where you will sign release forms and they will explain all the procedures on your receiving your prizes—both consolation and big winnings."

The entire group settled in their seats at that moment as the security issue was put to a short rest... and obviously the mention of *prizes* broke the intense silence.

TED: "On a more up note! I assume you all had a good night's sleep! Dreams filled with Q and A's, pressing the buzzer, and bonus points between the alpha waves. Well, let's go through the rules of the game one final time so we make sure every question is answered."

THE CONTESTANT COORDINATOR ON THE RULES OF THE GAME

Ted covered the format of the game and formally went down the list of rules. He was definitely talking to avid watchers of 'THE WIN OF YOUR LIFE'! My competitors were serious game players—it was definitely second nature to all of us. I was sure that they not only watched the game every day, but they had also set up a mock version of it in their living rooms.

TED: "Any questions, so far?"

I immediately opened up the floor: "Ted, my husband, Sid, is here today. He came with me from Ohio. I'd like him to visit me down on the set. Is that possible?"

TED: "Sally, we would all enjoy meeting Sid; but again, security disallows family or friends mingling with contestants on the set. If you win the bonus round, 'THE LIFETIME WIN,' then family and friends in the audience are invited down on to the set while the cameras are shooting the final minutes of the show...we want the public to share in your family's excitement. But moments after that you will be separated again until all game show business has been taken care of, such as prizes and more. I hope that answers your question."

Another contestant asked another very important question regarding the taping schedule. In summary, Ted explained that the two days of taping would consist of five shows today, and five shows tomorrow. If you win on the last taping today you come back tomorrow. If you don't tape today or tomorrow they will let you know your status tomorrow. If you win on the last taping tomorrow, the tenth show, you will come back for next week's two days of taping.

Then Ted gave his pep talk: "You're the cream of the contestant crop. Sitting in this room are the best of the best. I was involved in selecting you and when it comes to my contestants, modest I am not. And since you can't leave this room without me—security, remember?—you are going to hear my famous pep talk."

Ted was in rare form, or regular form, when one considers he interviews more than 15,000 potential contestants a year. I, as well as the other contestants, had big smiles on our faces as Ted delivered his pep talk. It was doing the trick. His clever routine covered ten steps on losing with dignity, the element of luck, smelling salts, spontaneity, deep breaths, gushing adrenaline, tuning out the cameras, untying tongues, stage fright, etc.

TED: "And if you start feeling that fear coming on, just make a mental picture of your living room—you're watching the show and again, your mother-in-law is vying for first crack at the answer...that'll bring you back to the competitive edge. It's like standing on the ledge of a building: Who in their right mind would look down? Don't focus on the cameras, the audience, the models, the yards of cables, or the lights. Focus on playing the game, the key reason you are here."

1:15. Makeup.

After pretaping touch-up and break-time, we, the "stars" of the show—the contestants—were ready for the cameras.

MARIAN THE HOST: "You all look great!"

Eyes lit up and heads turned as Marian entered the room with all her star power. The group was in awe.

MARIAN: "Are you all ready for your moment in lights? Just remember this is an *event* of your lifetime. You're here to play your favorite game and to come away with a wonderful memory. Don't take it too seriously. THE GAME IS NOT OVER UNTIL IT'S OVER! Keep with the game; even when your spirits are slipping...pull them back up. You want your home video to show a 'real' smile...because if it doesn't you'll know; you'll remember every time you watch it. Keep it in its proper perspective and remember: We're at our best when you're at your best. We are out for good television and you are the stars of the show. I'll see you on the set."

1:45. On the set of "The Win of Your Life."

This was Hollywood...the set of "The Win of

Your Life." Lights! Cameras! And the Action was everywhere. I was seated along with the rest of the group in the orchestra section of the studio audience seating area with the entire sound stage surrounding all of us. Network security was reiterating the seriousness of the issue and passed out the all-important and all-encompassing game show release form, requiring my signature, social security number, past game show experience, professional acting experience, acquaintance with network employees, etc.

I was amazed at its officiality.

- I am at least eighteen years of age.
- I am not (nor is any member of my immediate family) employed by or a close acquaintance of anyone employed by:
  (a) The production company, the network, their subsidiaries, or affiliates, or any television station that broadcasts the program.
  (b) To the best of my knowledge, any person, manufacturer or other firm supplying prizes to the program.
- I am not a candidate for public office and will not become a candidate before the broadcast of my appearance on the program.
- I have not been a contestant within the past year on any other television game show.
- The following are all of the television game shows on which I have appeared:

NAME OF SHOW:_____ DATE _____

NAME OF SHOW:_____ DATE _____

NAME OF SHOW:_____ DATE _____

The release form went on for three more pages. It covered every legal issue imaginable.

2:15. The Rehearsal.

TED: "It's time for the rehearsal game. The rehearsal is for you and for us. It's your opportunity to get comfortable with playing the game in this intense environment—in front of the cameras, under the hot lights, behind your podium. You get to practice pressing your sensitive buzzer, reading your questions on the huge playing board with its glaring lights, and responding to the director's cues. Your usual frame of reference is at your living room television set, sandwich in hand. 'On the set' is an intimidating circus.

"And we use your rehearsal as our last opportunity to reaffirm that you are the excellent game players we saw you as at your audition, with strong personalities able to cope with the pressures of exposure on national television. Let me reiterate why we chose you and what we want you to emphasize during your rehearsal:
• quick competitive reactions
• strong voice projection

- decisive category selection—plan your strategy before your turn arrives
- good sportsmanship—cheer your competitors on the same way you want your family in the audience to cheer you on. It's only natural to feel frustrated by a wrong answer; just don't show it. As Marian always says, 'You want your video memories to reflect the kind of good sportsperson you are. Remember, you're not performing brain surgery, you are playing a game.'

It's imperative that you are able to perform during the rehearsal. Look, if you pass out on us during your rehearsal, we might think twice about putting you on national television. Play your rehearsal as if you were playing for real dollars."

Somehow, all of us got through the rehearsal and the actual tapings began.

6:30. Fourth Taping.

TED: "Marsina and Jessian, you are the next contestants on 'The Win of Your Life' to play against our current champion. Please come down to the set."

My enthusiasm was still there but I was frustrated, wondering if I would go on today.

7:30 P.M. Fifth and Last Taping of the Day.

Ted approached the few remaining, anxiously awaiting contestants: "Jonerica and Sally, you are the next contestants to play 'The Win of Your Life' against our current champion. Please come down to the set."

I sprung out of my seat and I bounced on to the set with a nervous excitement that was very unfamiliar to me. They escorted me to my podium and just as I stepped up to it, the bright lights went on. They seemed so hot that I was worried that I wouldn't be able to concentrate. I was scared stiff. The cameras started to move about in front of me, to the side of me and everywhere. I didn't know if they had started or what. Then the announcer's voice came on, introducing the show and the host, Marian. Marian started the show interviewing me and the others. She asked me about my family and I talked about Sid, my husband, who was sitting in the audience; it was amazing how by talking about him and knowing that he was out there somewhere, my confidence started coming back. Then as the show began and Marian told us to grab our buzzers, mine started sliding in my hand…I had no idea my palms were sweating so much. As the board went into motion, my heart was in my throat, my knees were trembling. Marian asked the first question... I heard my name being called... I must have pushed the buzzer. I remember responding with something and feeling an emotional rush. Somehow I answered the question correctly and all I remember is that Marian said, "Good start, Sally. Proceed with the next choice. You're up to $100." My only explanation is that I know I knew my game and I must have been on automatic pilot from practicing so much. Something inside me must have had clicked on.

Whatever clicked on stayed on as I became a pro at the buzzer and a queen of the board. My $100 grew into $1,000 which grew into $5,000, then a trip to Tahiti, and $8,000 more big ones. But, what happened next I'll never understand to this day. It's one thing watching strangers on television; but it's a whole other crazy gambit standing in front of a camera being asked if you want to double or nothing.

8:30 P.M.
Sally risks it all!!!

MARIAN: "Congratulations, Sally, you have already won $13,000 and a trip to Tahiti, and now, you can take the money and run... or would you like to risk it all with the chance to double your winnings in the Bonus Round of Your Life! for a total of $26,000 and a trip around the world. Remember, regardless of what happens you still receive your year supply of press-on nails."

My stomach dropped. I don't know what it was, but I think it was my life flashing in front of my eyes. All I could think was that I had everything; but, nothing to lose...I came here with nothing so what did I really have to lose.

SALLY: "YES, my husband and I have always dreamed about a trip around the world."

TED JUST RECEIVED THIS POSTCARD...

Dear Ted,
South of France was beautiful, Greece was unbelievable. Can't wait for Japan. Sid remains in a state of shock watching me try to spend the whole $26,000. I can honestly say that "The Win of My Life" has been the best of my life. Thanks again!

Your worldwide friends,
Sally and Sid

CHAPTER

7

KNOW
YOUR
TALENT

"My first fan letter was from a woman in Harlem. She was in her sixties. She expressed her love for my work. It was the most incredible letter I have ever received."

> Dear Sam,
> I've never written a fan letter
> before, but after seeing you on the
> TV, I wanted to tell you what an
> inspiration you are. I don't think
> I've ever been touched in quite this
> way and I know you're going to be
> a big star...

"I wrote her back!"

"'Star Search' saw me in a club. They asked me to audition. The whole talent show competition was new to me. I knew I could get a good video out of it and I needed the money. They turned me down on the first audition. They told me I was too emotional for the public. But I didn't

Singer Sam Harris wearing "his heart on his sleeve" on "Star Search."

take no for an answer because I believed in the image I was projecting. Finally, they accepted me for who I was. My first show I came in my oversized tux, baggies, tennis shoes. This was the image I was creating for myself... it was me. The show said no and they kept trying to sway me. But I told them 'I'm wearing this.' I kept up the look. The audience saw me as I am. They watched me come up from a complete 'nobody situation' to something. When America watched—it was the American Dream. We're alike—we are both working and struggling. If I do well, they do well. I put my heart on my sleeve. Those twenty-five million people a week are there for life."

Where else can you be seen by twenty-five million viewers while performing your talent—without an agent, without being a member of a professional artist's union and without already being a "name"?

Sam Harris used the talent show as his vehicle to stardom and chopped a good five years off his career struggle. From a small club audience and constant nos on record deals, he went to the Motown label, twenty million fans, and being recognized by everyone—stardom.

WHAT'S *YOUR* TALENT?

Dancing	Song Writing
Singing	Playing an Instrument
Lip-Syncing	Delivering One-liners
Modeling	Leading Roles

HOW TO USE YOUR TALENT

Hold the music...before you two-step off to your prestardom audition, you must know the four break-a-leg essentials:

1) Know your talent show requirements.
2) Prepare for your audition.
3) Know how to make your audition appointment.
4) Reap the melodic rewards of being on a talent show!

CHOOSE YOUR TALENT SHOW

"DANCE FEVER"

"We are looking for dancing couples. Any style of dance is welcome."

—Paul Gilbert, Producer

Do you have the "hot feet" bug? Are you itching to shuffle off to Buffalo? Clean those jazz pants!

Polish those tap shoes! Now step out of your daily routine, on to the dance floor and into your feverish routine.

1) *"Dance Fever" requirements:*
- Age eighteen and over.
- Dance teams consisting of two people—male-male, female–female, or male-female.

2) *Prepare for your dance audition:*
- Select a dance partner—a friend, family member, someone from your aerobics or dance class
  a) with dance skills—rhythm and physical coordination
  b) with compatible working habits to yours—similar schedule for a long-term project (many hours will be needed), dedication and commitment to success, the winning attitude
  c) with compatible dance-movement rhythm to yours.
- For your dance number
  a) seek assistance from a local professional dancer, a dance instructor, or a choreographer. Be confident when you tell them your "Dance Fever" auditioning plans and demonstrate your talent
  b) select a musical arrangement, based on: 1) style of dance; 2) musical interests; 3)

Contestants compete for the Grand Prize on "Dance Fever."

Courtesy of Merv Griffin Enterprises and 20th Century–Fox Television

general audience appeal—upbeat material for the televison viewer. Remember you must hold the attention of fifty million viewers.

    c) Create your dance routine. Consider these factors to begin your project: 1) a solid, precise choreographed routine; 2) an exciting routine that will immediately capture and hold the audience's attention—a few sensational moves will *not* overcompensate for a weak routine; 3) remember—you will be judged by industry professionals. YOU MUST EXCITE THEM! 4) be unique in your creation. They see thousands of routines annually and they judge on originality.

    d) Costumes for your routine. Use these points as guidelines: 1) should complement each partner's figure; 2) should reflect the style of dance you are performing.

3) *Know how to make your audition appointment (see the Address for Success chapter for complete details on audition/ game show contact):*

● Setting up your audition: write or call "Dance Fever" requesting an audition appointment. There are auditions in Los Angeles and at a contestant search.

- Contestant Correspondence (*Note*: they prefer contact by mail): Dance Fever, Merv Griffin Enterprises, 1541 N. Vine Street, Hollywood, CA 90028, (213) 461-4701.

4) "Dance Fever"'s melodic rewards:

- Couples who appear on the show get a free trip to Los Angeles including airline, hotel, and general expenses.
- First appearance winnings: $1,000 per couple.
- Semi-final winnings: $5,000 per couple.
- Final winnings: cash and prizes totalling more than $50,000.

"PUTTIN' ON THE HITS"
"PUTTIN' ON THE KIDS"

"We look for original talent acts performed in the form of lip-syncing to pre-existing musical pieces. You become the star you always wanted to be."

    —Todd Denkin, Senior Contestant
      Coordinator

WANTED: Closet performers who imitate their favorite performers—and do it well. Take your living room performances and your fabulous uninhibited struts on the road to Hollywood!

A contestant's amazing dual imitation of
Lionel Richie and Diana Ross performing
"Endless Love" on "Puttin' On the Hits."

1) *"Puttin' On the Hits" and "Puttin' On the Kids" requirements:*
- "Hits"
  a) Age five and over (*Note*: ages five to thirteen are allowed on "Hits" only after they have won on "Kids")
  b) Lip-syncing individuals, couples, or groups—any combination of performers
- "Kids"
  a) Ages five to thirteen
  b) Lip-syncing individuals, couples, or groups—any combination of performers

2) *Prepare for your lip-sync audition:*
- Select the performer/performing group and one of their songs you want to lip-sync. Deciding factors:
  a) Knowledge of lyrics
  b) Ability to lip-sync well to the lyrics
  c) Song that allows the creation of a distinct character(s), whether it be an imitation of the original or an original on its own

Follow these Insider's Tips
  a) If you are imitating a pre-existing performer's or performing group's style, familiarize yourself with and incorporate his/her or their movements and choreography.
  b) If you are creating an original act to a pre-existing song, arrange a creative and dy-

namic choreographed routine based on the story line of the song. 1) Practice your act in front of a mirror; 2) make sure your act is fun to watch; 3) you must have good stage presence; 4) you must project confidence; 5) the length of your act should be one and a half minutes.

3) *Know how to make your audition appointment (see the Address for Success chapter for complete details on audition/game show contact):*

- Setting up your audition

  Call or write "Puttin' On the Hits" and "Puttin' On The Kids" requesting an audition appointment. There are auditions in Los Angeles and at a contestant search.

- Contestant Correspondence (*Note:* shows prefer contact by phone):

Puttin' On the Hits, Dick Clark Productions, Chris Bearde Productions, 3003 West Olive Avenue, Burbank, CA 91505, (818) 843-POTH.

Puttin' On the Kids, Dick Clark Productions, Chris Bearde Productions, 3003 West Olive Avenue, Burbank, CA 91505, (818) 843-KIDS

4) *"Puttin' On the Hits" melodic rewards:*

- Performers who appear on the show get an all-expenses-paid one-week trip to Los Angeles—airline, hotel, and general expenses

KNOW YOUR TALENT

- First appearance winnings: $1,000 per act
- Semi-final winnings: $5,000 per act
- Final winnings: $25,000 per act

"Puttin' On the Kids" melodic rewards:
- Performers who appear on the show get an all-expenses-paid-one-week trip to Los Angeles—airline, hotel, and general expenses
- First appearance winnings: $500 savings bond
- Semi-final winnings: $2,000 savings bond
- Finals: $5,000 savings bond

A colorful lip-syncing performance of "The Pointer Sisters."

A young "Freddie Jackson."

"Tina Turner" struts her stuff.

An adorable rendition of "It's My Party."

A Carmen Miranda imitator
of "Puttin' On The Kids."

A hysterical send-up of Waylon Jennings and Willie Nelson.

"DREAM GIRL, U.S.A."

"Our weekly beauty contest is open to all women eighteen to thirty, married or single, who are personable, outgoing, good looking and talented."
— Ernest Chambers, Coexecutive Producer

Do you have talent? looks? personality? latent fantasies of being a Miss/Mrs. America? If so, stop dreaming, girl . . . YOUR TIME HAS COME!

1) *"Dream Girl, U.S.A." requirements:*
- Ages eighteen to thirty
- Married or single
- One specific talent
- Good looks
- Good figure
- Outgoing personality

2) *Prepare for your pageant:*
- Your Talent—key points to consider:
  a) Target your talent—singing, dancing, dramatic reading, playing an instrument
  b) Develop your talent act to the best of your ability
  c) Contact a professional in the area of your talent for expertise

- Your Looks—key points to consider:
  a) Hair—a style that is most flattering to your face and the professional image you want to project as a "Dream Girl"
  b) Face—makeup that brings out your strong attractive features and deemphasizes any facial flaws
  c) Body—the pageant includes a swimsuit competition; therefore total body conditioning is important. Insider's Tips: dance classes, aerobic workouts, basic isometric exercises, swimming, jogging, weight lifting, other toning athletic activities.
  d) Fashion—current fashion awareness and participation
- Stage Presence—key points to consider:
  a) Speaking eloquently—practice talking about yourself to a group of people
  b) Walking with poise and grace (the old book on the head routine still works)
  c) Develop the ability to emanate your inner beauty and combine it with your external good looks
  d) Practice eye contact and exude energy
3) *Know how to make your audition appointment (See the Address for Success chapter for complete details on audition/game show contact):*

- Setting up your audition
  a) Write "Dream Girl, U.S.A." requesting an audition appointment. There are auditions in Los Angeles and at a contestant search
  b) Your written correspondence should also include this personal information: 1) date of birth, 2) height, 3) weight, 4) hair color, 5) eye color, 6) marital status, 7) number of children and their ages, 8) type of talent, 9) other pageant or talent show experience, and 10) occupation
- Contestant Correspondence:
  Dream Girl, U.S.A.
  Chambers-Seligman Productions
  P.O. Box 900
  Beverly Hills, CA 90213

4) "Dream Girl, U.S.A." melodic rewards:
- First round winnings: trip to tropical setting
- Semi-final winnings: grand piano and sports car
- Final winnings: $100,000 cash

A shining moment for another pageant winner.

Host Ken Howard with "Dream Girl, U.S.A." winner.

"YOU WRITE THE SONGS"

"Do you have proven song-writing skills? We are looking for songwriters whose songs have real commercial potential—a solid memorable hook, solid lyrics, good commercial melody, original theme and/or an idea with a broad mass appeal."
—Evan Greenspan, Song Coordinator

Don't let that tune escape your head! Don't discount that persistent melodic hum! Don't dawdle with that ditty...get it on tape. Practice prerecording for your big hit!

1) *"You Write the Songs" requirements:*
   - Age eighteen and over
   - Song writers can consist of individuals, partners, or groups
   - Original songs
   - Songs with commercial hit potential—professional qualities of lyrics, melody, and originality
   - Songs with contemporary pop style—i.e., Top 40, adult contemporary, rhythm and blues, country
   - Songs must not have appeared in the top one hundred singles ratings chart of any domestic or international major music industry publication

- Songs must not have been a part of an album charted in the top fifty of the pop album chart of any domestic or international music industry publication
- Lyric sheets must accompany all song submissions

2) Prepare your song for presentation:

- It must have
  - a) broad mass appeal
  - b) a commercial melody
  - c) solid lyrics
  - d) a strong hook
  - e) musical instrumental backing if you are not adept at an instrument
  - f) for professional assistance contact songwriter organizations, songwriting classes, and local songwriters
  - g) listen to your local commercial pop radio stations
  - h) watch television video shows

3) Know how to audition your song:

- Submit your songs by mail
  - a) on demo audiocassettes, properly identified with writer's name and contact information (*Note*: you may submit as many tapes/songs as you like, but only submit one song per cassette)
  - b) accompanied by lyric sheets for each song.
- Contestant Correspondence: You Write the

Songs, Bob Banner Associates, P.O. Box Song, 8033 Sunset Blvd., Los Angeles, CA 90046, (213) 652-1230 (telephone number is for information only)

4) "You Write the Songs" melodic rewards:

- ONE TELEVISION SEASON IN-CLUDES—
  a) regular competition programs (round one: weeks one to eleven; round two: weeks thirteen to twenty-four): three songs compete each week. Each song receives a judging score. The song receiving the highest score becomes that week's winning song and competes against two new songs in the following week's episode. Each week's winning song wins: $1,000
  b) final competition programs (round one: week twelve; round two: week twenty-five): At the end of each round of regular competition, a cumulative score will be calculated for each song appearing in that round. The five top-scoring songs from each round will compete in a special final competition episode. The final competition winning song will receive the amount combined with weekly winnings that will total $100,000.

"STAR SEARCH"

"Star potential!!! We want people with special qualities, personalities, with potential to become major *stars* in the entertainment industry. Dancers, singers, models, comedians, musical groups...STAR POTENTIAL...including people outside the entertainment industry who wouldn't have the opportunity to become one of tomorrow's stars on a regular basis."

—Eric Rollman, Talent Coordinator and
Michelle Butin, Associate Producer

Do the agents hang up? Do you want to keep your last name? Can't get in a union without a part? Can't get a part without being in a union? Tired of performing in local clubs? Want to try a *national club*? TELEVISION could be your answer.

1) "Star Search" requirements:
- Age
  a) Juniors division: up to twelve years
  b) Teens division: ages thirteen through seventeen
  c) Adults division: ages eighteen and over.
- Individuals, couples/partners, or groups for different categories of talent
  a) Juniors' categories of talent are dance and vocal

b) Teens' categories of talent are dance and vocal
c) Adults' categories of talent are dance, vocal, television spokesmodel, musical group, and stand-up comedy

2) Prepare for your talent audition:

"Star Search" looks for talented contestants who stand out from the rest, have commercial appeal, and emanate star quality.

There are five steps to developing a professional audition: 1. professional training, 2. performing style, 3. selecting the audition number/piece, 4. perfecting the "act," 5. developing the "look."

- Dance category

1. *Professional Training.* Well-rounded professional dance instruction in a variety of dance media (e.g., jazz, tap, ballet, modern). Contact the best dance classes in your area and inform them of your "Star Search" plans.

2. *Performing Style.* Select the dance medium that suits your talent and ability. Make sure that your style appeals to the masses of contemporary television audiences.

3. *Selecting the Dance Number.* Choose the musical accompaniment that corresponds with your style of dance. Keep it upbeat.

4. *Perfecting the "Act."* Present a precise choreographed routine. The act must be exciting enough to hold the audience's attention from the first two-step to the last shuffle. Incorporate a wide variety of dance steps. Be technically precise.

5. *Developing the "Look."* Your "look" should directly relate to your style of dance. Your costumes, makeup, and hairstyle should reflect the theme of the dance piece you are performing. Partners' costuming should complement each other.

- Vocal category

1. *Professional Training.* Seek vocal training in contemporary singing. Incorporate your selected style and song into your formalized training.

2. *Performing Style.* Pop, rhythm & blues, country, easy listening. Choose a vocal style that suits your present image, even before developing your "look." Don't try to be something you're not.

3. *Selecting the Song.* Top 40! Commercial appeal! Select the song that lends itself well to your voice. Make sure that you are performing a new and original version of a pre-existing successful song and performer. DO NOT IMITATE THE SUCCESSFUL ORIGINAL.

4. *Perfecting the "Act."* Sing with your coach. Sing in front of your friends, strangers, at a local club, local amateur nights. THIS IS NOT TO SAY THAT THE SHOWER SHOULD BE ELIMINATED.

5. *Developing the "Look."* Be discriminating with your appearance. It should reflect your style of singing. Don't assume that elaborate costumes, heavy makeup and exaggerated hairstyles will over-compensate for a lack of talent.

- Spokesmodel category

1. *Professional Training.* Obtain modeling experience through modeling classes, print and ramp work, catalog work, and Teleprompter training.

2. *Performing Style.* Create a personalized, current fashion image for yourself and project the image from within. Study the styles currently in vogue in magazines, television, movies, fashion shows, retail/wholesale fashion catalogs.

3. *Selecting the Audition Number.* Your style of walking, your poise, and your personal energy and sincerity are the key spokesmodel ingredients.

4. *Perfecting the "Act."* Practice walking a distance with a book on your head. Make sure your body is in good shape. Practice

reading off cue cards held by another party. Remember: The ability to read cold yet with an awareness of what you are saying is vital. Your voice should be well modulated and have a pleasing quality. And above all, maintain your appearance from the first until last day of taping.

5. *Developing the "Look."* Tantalize the audience with your makeup, physique, hairstyle, posture, walk and approach.

- Musical group category

1. *Professional training.* Seek professional training for your instrument.

2. *Performing Style.* Select a contemporary musical group "image" based on the category you are representing, e.g. rock and roll, soft rock, easy listening, country and western, heavy metal, rhythm and blues. Select a category with mass commercial appeal that you could and would like to visualize in a current video.

3. *Selecting the Audition Number.* Whether you choose an original composition or a current Top 40 hit, make sure that it's professional material and would appeal to fifty million viewers. Consult objective professionals on your selection.

4. *Perfecting the "Act."* Practice day in and day out! Your practice environment should

be private and free of interruptions. Local clubs are an excellent vehicle for measuring public appeal.

5. *Developing the "Look."* Each member's look should complement the overall "look" of the group and should reflect the style of the piece you're performing. THE GROUP SHOULD HAVE ONE COHESIVE IMAGE.

- Stand-up comedy category

  1. *Professional Training.* For your performance, take acting classes, learn voice dialects, and frequent stand-up comedy clubs. For your material, study other acts and develop your own personal style of writing.

  2. *Performing Style.* Develop a character (e.g., goofy, insecure, abrasive, lovable) and consistently maintain that character throughout your act.

  3. *Selecting the Comedy Routine.* Take familiar everyday situations and incorporate them into your "character." Your routine must have a beginning, middle, and end. It can be either a complete story line or several scenarios with an underlying theme.

  4. *Perfecting the "Act."* Practice makes funny! Use the mirror, use your friends, use strangers, use local clubs' amateur

nights—and make sure you're leaving them laughing. Be flexible with your material: If the laughs just aren't strong enough, change a word or two, experiment with your timing and delivery. BE AWARE OF YOUR AUDIENCE'S RESPONSE! PLAY WITH AND OFF YOUR AUDIENCE! CONNECT WITH YOUR CROWD.

5. *Developing the "Look."* What's your image? Your "look" should be a direct reflection of your character and material. BELIEVABILITY! Startle your audience with your comedic image. Be memorable!

3) *Know how to make your audition appointment!*

- Submit your talent by mail!

a) Each submission must include:

1. Cover letter outlining your talent, personal goals, and interest in appearing on "Star Search." Include all pertinent personal data.

2. Biography. List your performance experience and professional training.

3. 8 × 10 black-and-white photograph

4. Demo tape—audio or video—maximum length five minutes

5. References. Include names, addresses, and telephone numbers.

- Contestant Correspondence: Star Search, Bob Banner Associates, P.O. Box Star, 8033 Sunset Boulevard, Hollywood, CA 90046, (213) 652-7600 (telephone number is for information only).

4) "Star Search"'s melodic rewards:

Each week, two contestants/contestant teams compete against each other within each talent category. The winning contestant(s) from each category proceed to the next week to compete against new contestant(s)/challengers. All winnings prior to the Finals grand prize are based on the American Federation of Television and Radio Artists (AFTRA) performance payment scale, since weekly winnings are interpreted as earnings. AFTRA is the performing union for television and radio artists (affiliated with the AFL-CIO) that sets the financial parameters for this branch of the entertainment industry.

- Weekly competition earnings:
  The Adult, Teen, and Junior Divisions and their respective talent categories receive the current AFTRA payment scale earnings. (Note: for current payment scales contact AFTRA in Los Angeles at (213) 461-8111 or New York (212) 265-7700.

- Final competition winnings/last show of the season:

a) ADULTS—each talent category winner:
$100,000

b) TEENS—each talent category winner:
$10,000

c) JUNIORS—each talent category winner:
$10,000.

TODAY'S TALENT SHOW WINNERS ARE TOMORROW'S STARS

John Kassir appeared on "Star Search" as a stand-up comedian. Since "Star Search" he has:

- Costarred in an off-Broadway production of *Three Guys Naked From The Waist Down.*
- Been a regular on "First & Ten," the HBO miniseries.
- Hosted "TV 2000," the video variety show on USA Network.
- Starred in Diet Coke commercials.

Marcie Leeds appeared on "Puttin' On the Kids" as Donna Summer. Since her appearance on the show, she has

- Costarred in the made-for-television movie *When The Bough Breaks*, starring Ted Danson.

Janet Jones appeared on "Dance Fever." Since then, she has been:

- Chosen for the female lead in the movie *Flamingo Kid*, costarring with Matt Dillon.
- Chosen for the female lead in the movie *American Anthem*, costarring Mitch Gaylord.
- Become a member of Motion, the regular dance company on "Dance Fever."

Michael Jay and his song appeared on "You Write the Songs." His single, "Hot Summer Nights" was featured in the movie *Top Gun*.

Denise Vlasis appeared on "Puttin' On the Hits" as Madonna, and has since toured Japan imitating Madonna.

Debra Sandlund appeared on "Dream Girl, U.S.A." and has been cast in several major motion pictures.

Sawyer Brown, the musical group, appeared on "Star Search." They have
- Made a deal with Capital/Curb Records.
- Opened the Kenny Rogers International Tour.
- Been nominated for Favorite Country Video, Duo or Group by The American Music Awards, 1987.
- Won the Country Music Association's Hori-

zon Award for the year's group with the most career progress.

- Had a number one single in the United States on the country charts.

Billy Huffsey appeared on "Dance Fever" and now costars as Christopher Donlon on the television show "Fame."

Dana Rogers appeared on "Dream Girl, U.S.A." and is a host of a home shopping television show.

Misha Segal and Harriet Schock appeared on "You Write the Songs." Their single, "First Time On A Ferris Wheel" was released as a duet sung by Carl Anderson and Gloria Loring.

Tracy Ross appeared on "Star Search" as a spokesmodel. She has since appeared on the covers of numerous magazines and costars on the soap opera "Ryan's Hope."

MYTH...
UNDER-
STOOD

MYTH:

"I know I could become a contestant, because Sophie's nephew works with someone whose brother lives in Hollywood and has a girlfriend who interviews contestants on 'The Win of Your Life.' And she told me that they like tall blonds like me."

UNDERSTAND:

- Contestant selection is an objective process based on game-playing skills, personality attributes, test scores, and overall winning potential.
- Connections could work against you. Network security disallows close acquaintance with any employees or affiliates of a particular show.
- Game shows are interested in contestant contrast on each particular taping. They want any and all types of contestants who are potential winners—all races, occupations, backgrounds, ages, physical attributes, and personality traits.

MYTH:

"I'll bet you, you can't be on 'The Win of Your Life' because you won $9,000 on that game show in 1974. But, then again, I heard that if you don't put it on your application they'll never find out. ...You know the old saying, what they don't know won't hurt them."

UNDERSTAND:

- What they find out could hurt you! Network security and game shows can find out plenty regarding your previous game show experience. The game show industry works together in maintaining current files on each and every game show contestant to date.

- Each game shows has its own respective restrictions on contestants' previous game show experience, regardless of whether contestants were big winners or consolation winners. Rumors constantly fly in this area of game show myths. The best answer always comes from the most appropriate source. If you are a former contestant, when writing or calling for your game show audition ask, "How many prior game show appearances would disallow me from becoming a contestant on your show?" (See the Address for Success chapter for complete details.)

MYTH:

"What's the name of that show I'm going to audition for. . . . well whatever. Come on, with my personality I'll have no problem overcompensating for not having seen the show. I know if I jump up and down, give lots of phony smiles, schmooze with the contestant coordinators, I'll get on. Wow, imagine an all-expense-paid trip to Hollywood. Who can beat that even if I lose?"

UNDERSTAND:

- Game show contestant coordinators see hundreds of contestants a week from all over the country and in all parts of the country. We see through unprepared contestants very soon into the audition. Even the smartest can't overcompensate for lack of game-playing experience.

- Do you enjoy watching contestants jump up and down? Or do you need an aspirin everytime one does? What kinds of contestants do you cheer on at home? Current contestant selection criteria are very sophisticated. We look for people who are skilled at the game, have interesting personalities, and seem real to the viewing public.

- Do you really think that any auditionees who make it all the way to contestant status are really losers? You might not get an all-expense-paid trip to the taping; many shows don't cover this. But what the game shows do cover is winnings for all contestants, be it $1,000,000, a sports car, a new refrigerator or a lifetime supply of press-on nails. And don't forget, a lifetime memory—your fifteen minutes of stardom!

MYTH:

"Congratulations on winning...you're going to have to pay a fortune in taxes on your fifteen minutes of stardom. Game shows and the IRS ask for special payments from contestants. And as for that refrigerator, they said it was valued at $1,500. That's a pretty penny, but you'll be paying more in taxes than if you bought one like it at Appliance City."

UNDERSTAND:

- The cash and prizes you won as a contestant during one year are included as ordinary income in that same year's tax returns. At your tax preparation time:
  - a) Cash winnings are added to your income for the tax year.
  - b) Prize winnings are added to your income. The dollar value is based on the suggested retail price determined by the game show.

- However, if Appliance City or any other store, for that matter, has the exact same model of refrigerator at a lower retail price (not a sale price), it's considered fair market value. You are allowed to claim the fair market value as your prize winning(s) income for tax purposes, if, and only if you disclose proof of the value difference with that year's tax returns. (*Note:* Game shows file their own Tax Form 1099 on each contestant's winnings based on cash value for cash and suggested retail value on prizes. Therefore, we suggest that your backup proof on your fair market value tax information be solid.)

- Winning a prize does not mean that you are obligated to take it home to mother.

OPTIONS:

    a) Auction. It's your refrigerator now and you can sell it if you want at an established retail price based on your researched fair market value and the game show's suggested retail price. Understand, however, that any advertising to attract a customer cannot include the name of the game show on which you won the prize(s).

    b) Favorite charity. Charities welcome contestants' winnings. Understand that your winnings are still considered earned income and at the same time, the value of your donation is considered a "contribution deduction."

    c) Forfeiting. You can forfeit any part or all of your winnings—cash and/or prizes. Understand forfeiture means that your winnings have no effect whatsoever on your income taxes; it's as if you never won. The best time to decide to forfeit is at the time you win. If you can't decide then, we suggest you ask your game show for the decision deadline to properly forfeit your winnings.

Understand, however, that mother might be very upset if you sell it, give it away, or God forbid, forfeit it!

MYTH:

"So I go on a game show, win some money, win some appliances. But who really cares? Who really watches these game shows? I mean, I'm kind of embarrassed to tell anyone I'm going for the audition."

UNDERSTAND:

"My daughter saw me; she's almost three. She was sitting in front of the television just shocked. She kept saying, 'Mommie, Mommie, why are you on TV, you're sitting here watching TV with me.'"

 —Kym Joseph, winning contestant
 "The Price is Right"

"People call me constantly. They want interviews, newspapers want to do stories—it's a media circus! It changed my life! Everyone is recognizing me. Yesterday I was walking down the street and people, complete strangers, came over to me and said 'Hi, Chuck!'".

 —Chuck Forrest, winning contestant
 "Jeopardy!"

"I've been getting cards from New York to Chicago from relatives, and all kinds of letters and postcards from different people!"

 —Lawrence E. Adams, winning contestant
 "The Price is Right"

In fact, the attention you will receive will be so great that we suggest you practice reciting these affirmations:

"No, Aunt Milly, your sinus condition won't take the tropical climate... I thought you were happy with the press-on nails!"

"Of course I want to give you a ride in the new sports car, Gerard, but I'm all booked today... there's a few time slots open for tomorrow."

"How many cousin Harolds can one person have?"

ADDRESS
FOR
SUCCESS

Buzz in quick with your answers, please:

Have you targeted your game show?　　　YES

Do you know your game?　　　YES

Have you developed your most
potent personality?　　　YES

Then you are ready for your ADDRESS TO
SUCCESS!

Two ways to audition:
1) At the television studio in the city of taping.
Travel arrangements must be made.
2) Out-of-town contestant searches. It's like auditioning in your own backyard.

- The game show summaries in this chapter
list the shows that conduct contestant
searches.
- Watch *your* game show for contestant search
announcements.
- Watch the Sunday classified ads of your local newspaper.
- Send away for information on contestant
searches.
- Telephone for information making reference
to contestant searches (see "Three ways to
get in touch" below for details).

Three ways to get in touch—scheduling your audition appointment.

1) Calling for success. If the game show provides a telephone number use it for audition information and possibly an audition appointment. It is the fastest and surest way to reach your show.

A) Out-of-town contestants:

- For an audition at the TV studio, say something like: "Hi, my name is Sally Cheton and I am calling from Fernville, Ohio ... and I am planning a trip to Hollywood during the period of __.

  a) When will you be interviewing during that time?

  b) Will I be able to get through all my interviews during that time?

  c) If I qualify, will I be able to tape my shows during that time?"

- For an audition in your area—contestant search information by telephone:

  "Hi, my name is Sally Cheton and I am calling from Fernville, Ohio and I am interested in auditioning for your show. Will you be conducting a contestant search in or around my area in the coming months?"

  BE BRIEF AND TO THE POINT.

B) Local contestants:

  "Hi my name is Hannah Hollywood and I

am calling to make an audition appointment. When will you be interviewing? What is your audition process? How soon will I know?"
BE VERY POLITE AND TO THE POINT—DON'T WASTE THEIR TIME. YOU NEVER KNOW WHO IS AT THE OTHER END!

2) Address for success:

  A) Basic postcard requesting audition/interview appointment.

I WOULD LOVE TO BE A CONTESTANT ON
(your game show)
(name)
(street address) (apt./P.O. #)
(city) (state) (zip)
(telephone #: days)
(telephone #: eves)

THANK YOU VERY MUCH FOR CONSIDERING ME!
SINCERELY YOURS,
(your signature)

B) Basic postcard requesting information regarding contestant searches

---

I WOULD LIKE TO KNOW IF AND WHEN
YOU ARE CONDUCTING A CONTESTANT
SEARCH IN MY AREA.
(name)
(street address)   (apt./P.O. #)
(city) (state) (zip)

THANK YOU VERY MUCH FOR RESPONDING TO MY
CONTESTANT SEARCH REQUEST!
                    SINCERELY YOURS,
                    (your signature)

● THE FACE OF BOTH POSTCARDS: Use your
Address for Success correspondence addresses
in this chapter. Print or type your postcards.
Fill out your postcard as if your penmanship
were being scored. From the moment you
begin making contact with your game show,
your winning attitude should be very expli-

cit — even in your preliminary written correspondence.

3. Specialized Game Shows and Talent Shows
   • Refer to the chapter "Know Your Talent" for each specific show's requirements. One might want a portfolio, another might request a video. Details are very important with these types of shows.

FOUR UNIVERSAL GAME SHOW RULES: THE FOUR MUST KNOWS

1. You cannot appear on the same game or talent show twice in a lifetime; this does not include special events pertaining to your first appearance (i.e., tournament of losers, tournament of champions, etc.)

2. Security — you cannot know or be associated with in any way anyone that works for your show's network, the production company, their affiliates or their subsidiaries on an ongoing or current basis. (See the On the Set chapter for complete details.)

3. All contestants receive consolation prizes or a facsimile thereof — everyone's a winner!

4. You cannot be a current candidate for U.S. government office.

GAME SHOWS

Remember, you said Yes! Yes! Yes! Now, use the information provided to properly set up your audition appointment. BE PERSISTENT WITH YOUR WINNING ATTITUDE.

ADDRESS FOR SUCCESS — WORKSHEET

1. AUDITION DATE: ————————————

2. AUDITION TIME: ————————————

3. AUDITION ADDRESS: ————————

————————————————————

4. ANY SPECIAL AUDITION INSTRUCTIONS:

————————————————————

————————————————————

5. ANY SPECIAL AUDITION PROCEDURES:

————————————————————

————————————————————

6. DIRECTIONS TO THE STUDIO: ————

————————————————————

————————————————————

NAME OF GAME SHOW: Bumper Stumpers
CATEGORY: Word/Puzzle
FORMAT: Two teams each consisting of two contestants earn the chance to try to solve super stumper puzzles which are personalized license plates — fictional and real. Example: two personalized license plates are shown and a famous name is announced. Contestants must guess who they belong to and must figure out what they stand for or say.
WINNINGS: Cash
CONTESTANT CRITERIA/GUIDELINES
  A) Age Range: Eighteen and over
  B) Contestant Status: Two individuals — you must select your teammate prior to auditioning
  C) How many game shows prior to appearing on this show: Only one appearance on this show with one year since your last game show appearance within last year.
  D) Conducts Contestant Searches: None — possibly in future
  E) Special Weeks: None — possibly in future
  F) Special Contestant Practices:
    • Handicapped (i.e., wheelchair)
    • Meals on taping days
CONTESTANT CORRESPONDENCE:
  A) Contestant Address: Bumper Stumpers
                          20 Victoria Street
                          Suite 504
                          Toronto, Ontario
                          M5C 2N8
  B) Contestant Telephone: (416) 868-1365
  C) Game Show prefers: phone calls

HOW TO BECOME A GAME SHOW CONTESTANT

NAME OF GAME SHOW: Card Sharks

CATEGORY: Trivia/Quiz

FORMAT: Two contestants compete, answering three kinds of questions. If contestant answers the question correctly then he/she gets to play the cards. Object is to run cards across board calling higher or lower. Winning two games earns a trip to the money cards with a bonus round.

WINNINGS: Cash and prizes

CONTESTANT CRITERIA/GUIDELINES:

A) Age range: Eighteen to any age

B) Contestant status: Individuals

C) How many game shows prior to appearing on this show: Taped for Nighttime Show: No more than two game shows in the last five years, with one year since your last game show appearance.

Taped for Daytime Show: No more than two game shows prior to your appearance on this show, with one year since your last game show.

D) Conducts contestant searches: A variety of cities in the United States

E) Special weeks: Teens, kids

F) Special contestant practices:
  - Handicapped (i.e., blind, wheelchair)
  - Catered dinners on taping days

CONTESTANT CORRESPONDENCE:

A) Contestant address: Card Sharks
   Mark Goodson Prod.
   6430 Sunset Blvd.
   Hollywood, CA 90028

B) Contestant telephone: (213) 520-1234

C) Game show prefers: phone calls

NAME OF GAME SHOW: Chain Reaction
CATEGORY: Word/Puzzle
FORMAT: Two couples make up two teams with one celebrity per team; both teams compete against each other playing a common board and guessing the missing words in an eight-word chain.
WINNINGS: Cash and prizes
CONTESTANT CRITERIA/GUIDELINES:
A) Age range: Eighteen to any age
B) Contestant status: Couples: two individuals who are linked to each other in some way (i.e. coworkers, friends, relatives, married)
C) How many game shows prior to appearing on this show: No restrictions
D) Conducts contestant searches: No
E) Special weeks: None—possibly in future
F) Special contestant practices:
    ● Catered lunches on taping days
    ● Handicapped (i.e., wheelchair)
CONTESTANT CORRESPONDENCE:
A) Contestant address: Chain Reaction
                       Bob Stewart Productions
                       1717 N. Highland Ave.
                       Suite 807
                       Hollywood, CA 90028
B) Contestant telephone: None
C) Game show prefers: postcards

HOW TO BECOME A GAME SHOW CONTESTANT

NAME OF GAME SHOW: Classic Concentration
CATEGORY: Word/Puzzle
FORMAT: Two contestants compete by matching numbers on a board behind which are a series of prizes. Once numbers have been exposed, a rebus puzzle is revealed. First contestant to solve the puzzle is given the opportunity to play bonus round for a bonus prize.
WINNINGS: Cash and prizes
CONTESTANT CRITERIA/GUIDELINES:
A) Age Range: Eighteen and over
B) Contestant Status: Individuals
C) How many game shows prior to appearing on this show: No more than two game shows in the last ten years; with one year since your last game show appearance
D) Conducts Contestant Searches: None
E) Special Weeks: Possibly in Future
F) Special Contestant Practices:
  ● Handicapped (i.e., wheelchair)
  ● Dinners on taping days
CONTESTANT CORRESPONDENCE:
A) Contestant address: Classic Concentration
Mark Goodson Productions
6430 Sunset Boulevard
Hollywood, CA 90028
B) Contestant Telephone: (213) 856-0638
C) Game Show prefers: phone calls

NAME OF GAME SHOW: The All New Dating Game
CATEGORY: Personality
FORMAT: Panel of three males or females compete against
each other for a date with one member of the opposite sex
who is asking amusing questions from behind a parti-
tion—only voices are heard.
WINNINGS: A trip
CONTESTANT CRITERIA/GUIDELINES:
  A) Age range: Sixteen to any age
  B) Contestant status: Single individuals
  C) How many game shows prior to appearing on this
     show: No more than two game shows in the last ten
     years, with one year since your last game show
     appearance.
  D) Conducts contestant searches: No—possibly in the
     future
  E) Special weeks: Alumni, double dates, twins, older
     singles, younger singles, special guest stars
  F) Special contestant practices:
     • Catered snacks on taping days
CONTESTANT CORRESPONDENCE:
  A) Contestant address: The All New Dating Game
                         Chuck Barris Productions
                         Sunset-Gower Studios
                         1420 N. Beachwood Drive
                         Stage 7 - Box 9
                         Hollywood, CA 90028
  B) Contestant telephone: (213) 469-2662
  C) Game show prefers: phone calls

HOW TO BECOME A GAME SHOW CONTESTANT

NAME OF GAME SHOW: Double Dare
CATEGORY: Kids/Teens
FORMAT: Two teams consisting of two players; the teams dare each other to answer trivia questions. If you don't know the answer and think the other team doesn't have a clue, you can double dare. When questions get to double dare status the team double dared must answer question or take the physical challenge. The winning team runs an outrageous obstacle course for additional winnings.
WINNINGS: Cash and Prizes
CONTESTANT CRITERIA/GUIDELINES:
  A) Age range: Eleven to thirteen
  B) Contestant status: Two individuals; you must select your teammate prior to auditioning
  C) How many game shows prior to appearing on this show: No restrictions
  D) Conducts contestant searches: A variety of cities in the United States.
  E) Special weeks: Parents, celebrity
  F) Special contestant practices: None—possibly in future
CONTESTANT CORRESPONDENCE:
  A) Contestant address: Double Dare
                          1133 6th Avenue
                          28th Floor
                          New York, NY 10036
  B) Contestant telephone: (212) 944-3646
  C) Game show prefers: Letters. One of your school's teachers must first contact the show and recommend you for an audition.

NAME OF GAME SHOW: High Rollers
CATEGORY: Trivia/Quiz
FORMAT: Two contestants compete against each other answering questions. The first contestant who buzzes in and answers question correctly gets control of the dice. Contestant can roll them or pass. Object is to clear each of three columns scattered with numbers from one to nine—each column contains a prize. Winning two games constitutes a winner and one moves on to a bonus round—bonus is to clear all numbers off the entire board.
WINNINGS: Prizes and cash bonus
CONTESTANT CRITERIA/GUIDELINES:
A) Age Range: Eighteen and over
B) Contestant Status: Individual contestants
C) How many game shows prior to appearing on this show: No more than two game shows in the last ten years; with one year since your last game show appearance
D) Conducts Contestant Searches: None—possibly in future
E) Special Weeks: None—possibly in future—i.e. newlywed, brides' week, graduates
F) Special Contestant Practices:
● Dinner on taping days
CONTESTANT CORRESPONDENCE:
A) Contestant address: High Rollers
Merrill Heatter
Hollywood Center Studios
6601 Romaine Avenue
Hollywood, CA 90028
B) Contestant Telephone: (213) 469-4041
C) Game Show prefers: phone calls

HOW TO BECOME A GAME SHOW CONTESTANT

NAME OF GAME SHOW: Hollywood Squares
CATEGORY: Trivia/Quiz
FORMAT: Two contestants play tic-tac-toe with nine celebrities as guest panelists.
WINNINGS: Cash and prizes
CONTESTANT CRITERIA/GUIDELINES:
A) Age range: Eighteen to any age
B) Contestant status: Individuals
C) How many game shows prior to appearing on this show: No more than two game shows in the last five years, with one year since your last game show appearance.
D) Conducts contestant searches: Occasionally the show goes on the road and tapes in other states (i.e., Florida, Colorado)
E) Special weeks: None—possibly in future
F) Special contestant practices:
  • Contestants selected from studio audience for future taping day
  • Catered dinners on taping days
CONTESTANT CORRESPONDENCE:
A) Contestant address: Tickets
                       NBC
                       Burbank, CA 91523
  • request tickets for studio audience
B) Contestant telephone: (818) 840-4444 - NBC
  • request tickets for studio audience
C) Game show prefers: postcards

NAME OF GAME SHOW: Jackpot
CATEGORY: Trivia/Puzzle
FORMAT: Sixteen contestants remain on the program for one week. One contestant at a time is "King of the Hill" and the other contestants are holding riddles. The "King" calls on contestants one to fifteen and attempts to answer his/her riddle. When the "King" answers correctly he splits money with questioner. If the "King" is stumped by the questioner, he's replaced by him/her. "Kings'" questions accumulate money in the "Jackpot."
WINNINGS: Cash with bonus prizes
CONTESTANT CRITERIA/GUIDELINES:
A) Age range: Eighteen to any age
B) Contestant status: Individuals
C) How many game shows prior to appearing on this show: No more than two game shows, with one year since your last game show appearance.
D) Conducts contestant searches: No
E) Special weeks: None
F) Special contestant practices:
 • All sixteen contestants tape five shows
CONTESTANT CORRESPONDENCE:
A) Contestant address: Jackpot
 Bob Stewart Cable — The
 Global Television Network
 81 Barber Greene Road
 Toronto, Ontario
 Canada M3C 2A2
B) Contestant telephone: (416) 446-5311
C) Game show prefers: Phone calls

HOW TO BECOME A GAME SHOW CONTESTANT

NAME OF GAME SHOW: Jeopardy!

CATEGORY: Trivia/Quiz

FORMAT: Three contestants compete against each other providing questions to answers in one of six different categories. The game is played in three phases: Jeopardy, Double Jeopardy, and Final Jeopardy.

WINNINGS: Cash

CONTESTANT CRITERIA/GUIDELINES:

A) Age range: Eighteen to any age

B) Contestant status: Individuals

C) How many game shows prior to appearing on this show: No more than two game shows in the last five years, with one year since your last game show appearance.

D) Conducts contestant searches: Throughout the entire United States

E) Special weeks: Teen, senior, tournament of champions

F) Special contestant practices:
- Handicapped (i.e. wheelchair)
- Catered dinners on taping days
- All travel expenses are paid for contestants participating in Special Weeks

CONTESTANT CORRESPONDENCE:

A) Contestant address: Jeopardy!
Merv Griffin Enterprises
1541 N. Vine Street
Hollywood, CA 90028

B) Contestant telephone: (213) 466-3931

C) Game show prefers: no preference

NAME OF GAME SHOW: Love Connection
CATEGORY: Personality
FORMAT: One male or one female contestant has two appearances on the show. On the first appearance he or she selects a date with one out of three contestant panelists—members of the opposite sex. On the second appearance the audience tries to guess who he/she selected for a date. If the audience guessed a panelist other than dated panelist, then the selector has the option to go on another date, this time with the audience voted selectee.
WINNINGS: None—see "Special Contestant Practices" below
CONTESTANT CRITERIA/GUIDELINES:
  A) Age range: Twenty-three to any age
  B) Contestant status: Single individuals (cannot be a member of a professional actors' organization such as SAG, AFTRA, etc.
  C) How many game shows prior to appearing on this show: No restrictions
  D) Conducts contestant searches: No
  E) Special weeks: None
  F) Special contestant practices:
    • Complete date expenses are paid for
CONTESTANT CORRESPONDENCE:
  A) Contestant address: Love Connection
                          Lieber Productions
                          8601 Beverly Boulevard
                          Suite 5
                          Los Angeles, CA 90048
  B) Contestant telephone: (213) 659-6210
  C) Game show prefers: phone calls

HOW TO BECOME A GAME SHOW CONTESTANT

NAME OF GAME SHOW: Love Me, Love Me Not
CATEGORY: Personality
FORMAT: Three contestant panelists of the same sex attempt to deceive two contestants of the opposite sex reading whimsical statements concerning love and romance. Winning contestant and winning panelist contestant go on to bonus round.
WINNINGS: Cash and prizes
CONTESTANT CRITERIA/GUIDELINES:
A) Age range: Eighteen to forty
B) Contestant status: Individuals
C) How many game shows prior to appearing on this show: No restrictions
D) Conducts contestant searches: A few cities including Vancouver and Seattle
E) Special weeks: None
F) Special contestant practices:
  • Catered dinners on taping days
CONTESTANT CORRESPONDENCE:
A) Contestant address: Love Me, Love Me Not
                       Northstar Syndications, Inc.
                       585 16th St.
                       Suite 207
                       West Vancouver, BC
                       Canada V7V 3R8
B) Contestant telephone: (604) 925-2010
C) Game show prefers: postcards

NAME OF GAME SHOW: The New Newlywed Game

CATEGORY: Personality

FORMAT: Four newly married couples competing against each other. The respective new spouses' spontaneous answers to amusing questions test how well they know each other.

WINNINGS: Prize—contestants are asked prior to the show what type of prize they would like to win.

CONTESTANT CRITERIA/GUIDELINES:

A) Age range: Eighteen to any age

B) Contestant status: Newlywed couples (married two years or less)

C) How many game shows prior to appearing on this show: No more than two game shows in the last ten years, with one year since your last game show appearance.

D) Conducts contestant searches: No

E) Special weeks: Alumni, seniors, other special theme weeks

F) Special contestant practices:
   - Catered snacks on taping days

CONTESTANT CORRESPONDENCE:

A) Contestant address: The New Newlywed Game
   Chuck Barris Productions
   Sunset-Gower Studios
   1420 N. Beachwood Drive
   Stage 7 - Box 9
   Hollywood, CA 90028

B) Contestant telephone: (213) 469-4907

C) Game show prefers: phone calls

HOW TO BECOME A GAME SHOW CONTESTANT

NAME OF GAME SHOW: The $100,000 Pyramid
CATEGORY: Word/Puzzle
FORMAT: Two teams compete against each other; each team consists of a contestant and a celebrity. Each team is given a list of seven words from a category. The object is to get your partner to guess the words by using clue words or phrases. The winning team goes to the "pyramid" where one partner must give a list of things that pertain to a category and the other partner must guess the category these things belong to.
WINNINGS: Cash with bonus prizes
CONTESTANT CRITERIA/GUIDELINES:
A) Age range: Eighteen to any age
B) Contestant status: Individuals
C) How many game shows prior to appearing on this show: No more than two game shows, with one year since your last game show appearance.
D) Conducts contestant searches: No
E) Special weeks: Approximately every six to ten weeks there is a Special Tournament for $100,000
F) Special contestant practices:
  • Catered dinners on taping days
  • Handicapped (i.e., wheelchair)
CONTESTANT CORRESPONDENCE:
A) Contestant address: $100,000 Pyramid
                                 Bob Stewart Productions
                                 1717 N. Highland Ave.
                                 Suite 605
                                 Hollywood, CA 90028
B) Contestant telephone: (213) 461-3746
C) Game show prefers: phone calls

NAME OF GAME SHOW: The $1,000,000 Chance of a Lifetime

CATEGORY: Word/Puzzle

FORMAT: Two couples competing against each other; one spouse from each couple competes against each other while playing against the board trying to solve a word-puzzle, typically in the form of a phrase. The couple who wins three games and has the most money plays the bonus round.

WINNINGS: Cash and prizes

CONTESTANT CRITERIA/GUIDELINES:

A) Age range: Eighteen to any age

B) Contestant status: Married couples

C) How many game shows prior to appearing on this show: No more than two game shows in the last five years, with one year since your last game show appearance.

D) Conducts contestant searches: No

E) Special weeks: None

F) Special contestant practices:
  • Catered dinners on taping days

CONTESTANT CORRESPONDENCE:

A) Contestant address: The $1,000,000 Chance of a Lifetime
   Lorimar-Telepictures
   5842 Sunset Boulevard
   Building 11
   Hollywood, CA 90028

B) Contestant telephone: (213) 465-7391

C) Game show prefers: phone calls

HOW TO BECOME A GAME SHOW CONTESTANT

NAME OF GAME SHOW: The Price is Right
CATEGORY: Trivia/Quiz
FORMAT: Contestants are chosen from an audience to play an "On-Stage" game where they try to "guesstimate" price points on products with hopes of winning the showcase.
WINNINGS: Cash and prizes
CONTESTANT CRITERIA/GUIDELINES:

A) Age range: Eighteen to any age
B) Contestant status: Individuals
C) How many game shows prior to appearing on this show: No more than two game shows, with one year since your last game show appearance.
D) Conducts contestant searches: No
E) Special weeks: None
F) Special contestant practices:
   • Contestants selected from studio audience for same-day game playing

CONTESTANT CORRESPONDENCE:

A) Contestant address for tickets:
   The Price is Right
   CBS
   7800 Beverly Blvd.
   Los Angeles, CA 90036
   Attn: Ticket Dept.

B) Contestant telephone: None

C) Game show prefers:
   Write in or you may pick up tickets for same day taping if available.
   Pick-up address:
   CBS — (213) 460-3000
   7800 Beverly Boulevard (at Fairfax Avenue)
   Los Angeles, CA 90036
   at the CBS ticket window

NAME OF GAME SHOW: Sale of the Century
CATEGORY: Trivia/Quiz
FORMAT: Contestants compete by answering trivia questions, earning the chance to buy prizes at a fraction of their actual retail values.
WINNINGS: Cash and prizes
CONTESTANT CRITERIA/GUIDELINES:
A) Age range: Eighteen to any age
B) Contestant status: Individuals
C) How many game shows prior to appearing on this show: No more than two game shows in the last ten years, with one year since your last game show appearance.
D) Conducts contestant searches: No
E) Special weeks: Tournament of champions
F) Special contestant practices:
  ● Catered dinners on taping days
CONTESTANT CORRESPONDENCE:
A) Contestant address: Sale of the Century
     Reg Grundy Productions
     9911 W. Pico Blvd.
     Suite 720
     Los Angeles, CA 90035
B) Contestant telephone: (213) 284-8644
C) Game show prefers: phone calls

HOW TO BECOME A GAME SHOW CONTESTANT

NAME OF GAME SHOW: Scrabble
CATEGORY: Word/Puzzle
FORMAT: Two contestants compete against each other trying to guess word clues to solve a puzzle; first contestant to complete three words successfully moves on to play sprint—a bonus round. If sprint is won a certain number of times in a row the contestant wins big money.
WINNINGS: Cash
CONTESTANT CRITERIA/GUIDELINES:
A) Age range: Eighteen to any age
B) Contestant status: Individuals
C) How many game shows prior to appearing on this show: No more than two game shows in the last ten years, with one year since your last game show appearance.
D) Conducts contestant searches: Several cities in the United States including Detroit, Boston, Dallas, Chicago, Minneapolis, New York City, Atlanta, Philadelphia
E) Special weeks: Teen, college
F) Special contestant practices:
   • Catered lunches on taping days
   • Transportation to and from hotels for out-of-town contestants
   • Handicapped (i.e., wheelchair)

CONTESTANT CORRESPONDENCE:
A) Contestant address: Scrabble
   Reg Grundy Productions
   P.O. Box 67519
   Los Angeles, CA 90067
B) Contestant telephone: (213) 284-8644
C) Game show prefers: phone calls

NAME OF GAME SHOW: Split Second
CATEGORY: Trivia/Quiz
FORMAT: Three contestants compete against each other in three rounds. In rounds one and two contestants answer three-part questions that are shown on a screen. First contestant to buzz in has first choice of which part of the question they choose to answer. The remaining two parts of the question are left for opponents. Strategy is to buzz in first to select easier questions and therefore leaving harder ones for opponents. Round three is countdown round where leading contestants are required to answer less questions. Final winner moves on to bonus round.
WINNINGS: Cash and Grand prize
CONTESTANT CRITERIA/GUIDELINES:
A) Age Range: Eighteen and over
B) Contestant Status: Individuals
C) How many game shows prior to appearing on this show: Only one appearance on this year with two years since your last game show appearance.
D) Conducts Contestant Searches: None — possibly in future
E) Special Weeks: None
F) Special Contestant Practices:
   ● Meal on taping day
CONTESTANT CORRESPONDENCE:
A) Contestant Address: Split Second
   Hatos Hall Productions
   180 Bloor St West
   Toronto, Ontario
   M5S 2V6
B) Game Show prefers: Postcards only

HOW TO BECOME A GAME SHOW CONTESTANT

NAME OF GAME SHOW: Super Password
CATEGORY: Word/Puzzle
FORMAT: Two teams, each team consisting of two people, one celebrity and one contestant; the players must communicate "passwords" by giving one-word clues, then solve puzzles formed by these passwords.
WINNINGS: Cash
CONTESTANT CRITERIA/GUIDELINES:
A) Age range: Eighteen to any age
B) Contestant status: Individuals
C) How many game shows prior to appearing on this show: No more than two game shows in the last ten years, with one year since your last game show appearance.
D) Conducts contestant searches: No
E) Special weeks: Tournament of losers, tournament of champions
F) Special contestant practices:
   • Catered dinners on taping days
   • Handicapped (i.e., wheelchair)
CONTESTANT CORRESPONDENCE:
A) Contestant address: Super Password
                       Mark Goodson Productions
                       6430 Sunset Blvd.
                       Hollywood, CA 90028
B) Contestant telephone: (213) 466-5103
C) Game show prefers: phone calls

NAME OF GAME SHOW: Truth or Consequences
CATEGORY: Personality
FORMAT: Excuse game—the goal of the game is to get to the consequence. Contestants are asked questions they know they're not going to answer correctly because they know it's a trick question—a Catch-22. So they suffer the consequences.
WINNINGS: Cash and prizes
- Winnings are commensurate with the consequence suffered

CONTESTANT CRITERIA/GUIDELINES:
A) Age range: Any age
B) Contestant status: Individuals
C) How many game shows prior to appearing on this show: No more than two game shows, with one year since your last game show appearance.
D) Conducts contestant searches: Cities including New York, Chicago, San Francisco, Philadelphia and others
E) Special weeks: Yes
F) Special contestant practices:
- In addition to advance selection of contestants, contestants are also selected from studio audience for that same show's taping
- Handicapped (i.e., wheelchair, blind)
- In some cases, travel and hotel expenses

CONTESTANT CORRESPONDENCE:
A) Contestant address: Truth or Consequences; 1717 N. Highland Ave.; 9th Floor; Hollywood, CA 90028
(*Note:* Groups or organizations are welcomed as studio audience; if you are associated with one, state the name on your postcard.)
B) Contestant telephone: (213) 460-4414
C) Game show prefers: no preference

HOW TO BECOME A GAME SHOW CONTESTANT

NAME OF GAME SHOW: $25,000 Pyramid
CATEGORY: Word/Puzzle
FORMAT: Two teams compete against each other; each team consists of a contestant and a celebrity. Each team is given a list of seven words from a category. The object is to get your partner to guess the words by using clue words or phrases. The winning team goes to the "pyramid" where one partner must give a list of things that pertain to a category and the other partner must guess the category these things belong to.
WINNINGS: Cash with bonus prizes
CONTESTANT CRITERIA/GUIDELINES:
A) Age range: Eighteen to any age
B) Contestant status: Individuals
C) How many game shows prior to appearing on this show: No more than two game shows, with one year since your last game show appearance.
D) Conducts contestant searches: No
E) Special weeks: Teen, blind
F) Special contestant practices:
- Catered dinners on taping days
- Handicapped (i.e., blind)

CONTESTANT CORRESPONDENCE:
A) Contestant address: $25,000 Pyramid
Bob Stewart Productions
1717 N. Highland Ave.
Suite 605
Hollywood, CA 90028
B) Contestant telephone: (213) 461-3746
C) Game show prefers: phone calls

NAME OF GAME SHOW: Wheel of Fortune
CATEGORY: Word/Puzzle
FORMAT: Three contestants in turn spin a giant wheel, which stops on either cash amounts, a lost turn, or bankruptcy. When the wheel halts at a cash amount, the contestant guesses letters in a word puzzle. The same contestant may keep spinning the wheel accumulating cash, until he/she either lands on a noncash area, guesses a letter not included in the puzzle, or makes an incorrect attempt at solving the puzzle. The first contestant to correctly guess the puzzle goes on an in-studio "shopping spree" with his/her accumulated cash.
WINNINGS: Prizes
CONTESTANT CRITERIA/GUIDELINES:
A) Age range: Eighteen to any age
B) Contestant status: Individuals
C) How many game shows prior to appearing on this show: Taped for nighttime show: No more than two game shows, with one year since your last game show appearance
   Taped for daytime Show: No more than two game shows in the last ten years, with one year since your last game show appearance.
D) Conducts contestant searches: Throughout the entire United States
E) Special weeks: Teen, college, couples, celebrity
F) Special contestant practices:
   • Catered dinner on taping days
CONTESTANT CORRESPONDENCE:
A) Contestant address: Wheel of Fortune, Merv Griffin Enterprises, 1541 N. Vine Street, Hollywood, CA 90028
B) Contestant telephone: (213) 520-5555
C) Game show prefers: No preference

HOW TO BECOME A GAME SHOW CONTESTANT

NAME OF GAME SHOW: Win, Lose or Draw
CATEGORY: Personality
FORMAT: Two teams compete — a male team and a female team. Each team consists of two contestants and one celebrity; three players per team. The game is played like charades with the key difference in terms of drawing sketches rather than acting them out. The goal is for one member of a team to draw a sketch and two teammates attempt to guess the phrase while playing against the clock. If they are unable to guess, the opposing team has opportunity to guess. Both teams play in a similarly played bonus round.
WINNINGS: Cash
CONTESTANT CRITERIA/GUIDELINES:
  A) Age Range: Eighteen and over
  B) Contestant Status: Individuals
  C) How many game shows prior to appearing on this show: No more than two game shows prior to appearing on this show; with one year since your last game show appearance.
  D) Conducts Contestant Searches: Yes
  E) Special Weeks: None — possibly in future
  F) Special Contestant Practices:
    • Meals on taping days
CONTESTANT CORRESPONDENCE:
  A) Contestant address: Win, Lose or Draw
                         3855 Lankershim Blvd
                         North Hollywood, CA
                         91604
  B) Game Show prefers: Postcards Only

NAME OF GAME SHOW: WordPlay
CATEGORY: Word/Puzzle
FORMAT: Two contestants and three celebrities play a nine-word board. The contestants compete by selecting a word from the board. All three celebrities give their definitions of the word using comedy material with only one celebrity's definition being correct. If the contestant selects the correct celebrity's definition he wins the dollar amount of the word. The winning contestant proceeds to the bonus round.
WINNINGS: Cash and bonus prize
CONTESTANT CRITERIA/GUIDELINES:
A) Age range: Eighteen and over
B) Contestant status: Individuals
C) How many game shows prior to appearing on this show: No more than two game shows in the last ten years, with one year since your last game show appearance.
D) Conducts contestant searches: possibly in the future
E) Special weeks: possibly in future
F) Special contestant practices:
   • Catered dinner on taping days
   • Handicapped (i.e., wheelchair)
CONTESTANT CORRESPONDENCE:
A) Contestant address: WordPlay
   105 W. Alameda
   Suite 130
   Burbank, CA 91502
B) Contestant telephone: (818) 569-3664
   (818) 569-3665
C) Game show prefers: phone calls

TALENT SHOWS

Know your talent, target your talent show and follow the Audition Requirements. BREAK A LEG!

NAME OF TALENT SHOW: Dance Fever
FORMAT: Contestants compete in dance performances from ballroom dancing to current dance fads.
WINNINGS: Cash and prizes
CONTESTANT CRITERIA/GUIDELINES:
  A) Age range: Eighteen to any age
  B) Contestant status: Couples
  C) How many talent shows prior to appearing on this show: No restrictions
  D) Conducts contestant searches: More than seventy-five cities throughout the entire United States; cities outside the United States include: Copenhagen, Frankfurt, Rio de Janeiro, Manila, Mexico City, Freeport (Bahamas), Paris, Jamaica and others
  E) Special contestant practices:
    • All travel expenses are paid for contestants
CONTESTANT CORRESPONDENCE:
  • SPECIAL AUDITION REQUIREMENTS—for complete audition details see the Know Your Talent chapter.
  A) Contestant address: Dance Fever
                         Merv Griffin Enterprises
                         1541 N. Vine Street
                         Hollywood, CA 90028
  B) Contestant telephone: (213) 461-4701
  C) Show prefers: contact by mail

NAME OF TALENT SHOW: Dream Girl, U.S.A.

FORMAT: Female contestants compete in a pageant combining three major elements: 1) beauty, 2) talent, and 3) personality

WINNINGS: Cash and prizes

CONTESTANT CRITERIA/GUIDELINES:

A) Age range: Eighteen to thirty

B) Contestant status: Female individuals—United States citizens

C) How many talent shows prior to appearing on this show: No restrictions

D) Conducts contestant searches: In approximately fifty to sixty cities throughout the United States

E) Special contestant practices:
   • All travel expenses are paid for contestants

CONTESTANT CORRESPONDENCE:

• SPECIAL AUDITION REQUIREMENTS—for complete audition details see the Know Your Talent chapter.

A) Contestant address: Dream Girl, U.S.A.
   Chambers-Seligman
   Productions
   P.O. Box 900
   Beverly Hills, CA 90213

B) Contestant telephone: None

HOW TO BECOME A GAME SHOW CONTESTANT

NAME OF TALENT SHOW: Puttin' On The Hits
FORMAT: Contestants perform original talent acts in the form of lip-sync to pre-existing musical pieces.
WINNINGS: Cash
CONTESTANT CRITERIA/GUIDELINES:
 A) Age range: Five to any age
 B) Contestant status: Individuals, couples, and groups
 C) How many talent shows prior to appearing on this show: One year since your last game or talent show appearance
 D) Conducts contestant searches: Several cities throughout the U.S. including: Chicago, Miami, Phoenix, New York City, Detroit, Dallas, Tulsa, Cincinnati, Cleveland, Louisville
 E) Special contestant practices:
   • All travel expenses paid—one week in Los Angeles
   • All transportation to and from the studio
CONTESTANT CORRESPONDENCE:
   • SPECIAL AUDITION REQUIREMENTS—for complete audition details see the Know Your Talent chapter.
 A) Contestant address: Puttin' On the Hits
     Dick Clark Productions
     Chris Bearde Productions
     3003 West Olive Avenue
     Burbank, CA 91505
 B) Contestant telephone: (818) 843-POTH
 C) Talent show prefers: phone calls

ADDRESS FOR SUCCESS

NAME OF TALENT SHOW: Puttin' On The Kids
FORMAT: Contestants perform original talent acts in the form of lip-sync to pre-existing musical pieces.
WINNINGS: Cash
CONTESTANT CRITERIA/GUIDELINES:
A) Age range: Five to thirteen
B) Contestant status: Individuals, couples, and groups
C) How many talent shows prior to appearing on this show: One year since your last game or talent show appearance
D) Conducts contestant searches: Several cities throughout the U.S. including: Chicago, Miami, Phoenix, New York City, Detroit, Dallas, Tulsa, Cleveland, Cincinnati, Louisville
E) Special contestant practices:
   • All travel expenses paid—one week in Los Angeles
   • All transportation to and from the studio
CONTESTANT CORRESPONDENCE:
   • SPECIAL AUDITION REQUIREMENTS—for complete audition details see the Know Your Talent chapter.
A) Contestant address: Puttin' On the Kids
                       Dick Clark Productions
                       Chris Bearde Productions
                       3003 West Olive Avenue
                       Burbank, CA 91505
B) Contestant telephone: (818) 843-KIDS
C) Talent show prefers: phone calls

HOW TO BECOME A GAME SHOW CONTESTANT

NAME OF TALENT SHOW: Star Search

FORMAT: Contestants perform their talent selected from different musical variety, entertainment categories and compete against other contestants in the same talent category.

WINNINGS: Cash

CONTESTANT CRITERIA/GUIDELINES:

A) Age range: Any age
   Three categories: 1) Juniors, up to twelve, 2) Teens, thirteen to seventeen, and 3) Adults, eighteen to any age

B) Contestant status: Individuals, couples, and groups

C) How many talent shows prior to appearing on this show: No restrictions

D) Conducts contestant searches: U.S. cities include: Minneapolis, New York City, Dallas, Miami, Houston, Atlanta, Las Vegas, Nashville, Honolulu
   Cities outside the U.S. include: London, Manchester, Milan, Paris, Toronto, Montreal

E) Special contestant practices:
   ● All travel expenses paid for contestants
   ● Winning contestants automatically qualify for professional actors' unions (i.e. SAG, AFTRA)

CONTESTANT CORRESPONDENCE:

● SPECIAL AUDITION REQUIREMENTS—for complete audition details see the Know Your Talent chapter.

A) Contestant address: Star Search, Bob Banner Associates, P.O. Box Star,
   8033 Sunset Boulevard,
   Hollywood, CA 90046

B) Contestant telephone: (213) 652-7600
   recorded information only

C) Talent show prefers: contact by mail

NAME OF TALENT SHOW: You Write the Songs

FORMAT: A song writing show where contestant song-writers' compositions are in competition against one another; the competing songs are performed by established singers.

WINNINGS: Cash

CONTESTANT CRITERIA/GUIDELINES:

A) Age range: Eighteen to any age

B) Contestant status: Individuals, partners, and groups

C) How many talent shows prior to appearing on this show: No restrictions

D) Conducts contestant searches: No

E) Special contestant practices:
- All travel expenses are paid for contestants
- Handicapped (i.e. blind, wheelchair, and more)

CONTESTANT CORRESPONDENCE:

- SPECIAL AUDITION REQUIREMENTS—for complete audition details see the Know Your Talent chapter.

A) Contestant address: You Write the Songs
   Bob Banner Associates
   P.O. Box Song
   8033 Sunset Blvd.
   Los Angeles, CA 90046

B) Contestant telephone: (213) 652-1230

C) Talent show prefers: contact by mail

ABOUT THE AUTHORS

Greg Muntean: After graduating from college in Ohio, Greg accepted a position with Merv Griffin Enterprises in 1979 as the mailroom clerk. He worked his way up the ladder and became contestant coordinator for "Wheel of Fortune" in 1981. He served in this capacity until 1984 when he moved over to "Jeopardy!" as contestant coordinator, where he remains today.

Gregg Silverman: Gregg is the creator of a national innovation for the relocation industry and is the owner of a Southern California relocation company. He holds a degree in psychology and hails from Southern California.